T0257123

Practical Weak Supervision
Doing More with Less Data

Wee Hyong Tok, Amit Bahree, and Senja Filipi

Beijing · Boston · Farnham · Sebastopol · Tokyo

Practical Weak Supervision

by Wee Hyong Tok, Amit Bahree, and Senja Filipi

Copyright © 2022 Wee Hyong Tok, Amit Bahree, and Senja Filipi. All rights reserved.

Published by O'Reilly Media, Inc., 1005 Gravenstein Highway North, Sebastopol, CA 95472.

O'Reilly books may be purchased for educational, business, or sales promotional use. Online editions are also available for most titles (*http://oreilly.com*). For more information, contact our corporate/institutional sales department: 800-998-9938 or *corporate@oreilly.com*.

Acquisitions Editor: Rebecca Novack
Development Editor: Jeff Bleiel
Production Editor: Kristen Brown
Copyeditor: nSight, Inc.
Proofreader: Piper Editorial Consulting, LLC

Indexer: Ellen Troutman-Zaig
Interior Designer: David Futato
Cover Designer: Karen Montgomery
Illustrator: Kate Dullea

October 2021:   First Edition

Revision History for the First Edition
2021-09-30:   First Release

See *http://oreilly.com/catalog/errata.csp?isbn=9781492077060* for release details.

978-1-492-07706-0

[LSI]

Table of Contents

Foreword by Xuedong Huang

In specific industry scenarios AI systems can be brittle, and they often require heavy customization with lots of additional data to build machine learning models that help solve for those specific scenarios. However, with diverse data points, and the ability to combine these disparate data types together, there are new opportunities to pretrain machine learning models that are foundational to the downstream workloads. These models often require much less supervision for customization allowing for greater speed and agility at lower cost.

Transfer learning is a winning approach when combined with weak supervision. The foundational model can be strengthened with amazing gains. For example, when looking at very large pretrained speech, NLP, and computer vision models, weak supervision from big data can often produce a competent and sufficient quality allowing one to further compensate for limited data in the downstream task.

Finally, when building AI systems, one key challenge is to understand and act on user engagement signals. These signals are dynamic and weak by their nature. Combining weak supervision and reinforcement learning enables AI systems to learn which actions can solve for which tasks. The result is a high-quality dataset and an optimized model.

Over the last 30 years, I have had the privilege of working with many world-class researchers and engineers in creating what the world now sees as Microsoft's Azure AI services. Amit Bahree, Senja Filipi, and Wee Hyong Tok are some of my amazing colleagues who have dealt with practical AI challenges in serving our customers. In this book, they show techniques for weak supervision that will benefit anyone involved in creating production AI systems.

I hope you enjoy this book as much as I have. Amit, Senja, and Wee Hyong show us a practical approach to help address many of the AI challenges that we face in the industry.

— Xuedong Huang
Technical Fellow and Azure AI CTO, Microsoft
Bellevue, WA
September 2021

Foreword by Alex Ratner

The real-world impact of artificial intelligence (AI) has grown substantially in recent years, largely due to the advent of deep learning models. These models are more powerful and push-button than ever before—learning their own powerful, distributed representations directly from raw data with minimal to no manual feature engineering across diverse data and task types. They are also increasingly commoditized and accessible in the open source.

However, deep learning models are also more data hungry than ever, requiring massive, carefully labeled *training datasets* to function. In a world where the latest and greatest model architectures are downloadable in seconds and the powerful hardware needed to train them is a click away in the cloud, access to high-quality labeled training data has become a major differentiator across both industry and academia. More succinctly, we have left the age of model-centric AI and are entering the era of *data-centric AI*.

Unfortunately, labeling data at the scale and quality required to train—or "supervise" —useful AI models tends to be both expensive and time-consuming because it requires manual human input over huge numbers of examples. Person-years of data labeling per model is not uncommon, and when model requirements change—say, to classify medical images as "normal," "abnormal," or "emergent" rather than just "normal" or "abnormal"—data must often be relabeled from scratch. When organizations are deploying tens, hundreds, or even thousands of ML models that must be constantly iterated upon and retrained to keep up with ever-changing real-world data distributions, hand-labeling simply becomes untenable even for the world's largest organizations.

For the new data-centric AI reality to become practical and productionized, the next generation of AI systems must embody three key principles:

Data as the central interface
> Data—and specifically, training data—is often the key to success or failure in AI today; it can no longer be treated like a second-class citizen. Data must be at the center of iterative development in AI, and properly supported as the key interface to building and managing successful AI applications.

Data as a programmatic interface
> For data to be the center point of AI development, we must move beyond the inefficient status quo of labeling and manipulating it by hand, one data point at a time. Users must be able to develop and manage the training data that defines AI models *programmatically*, like they would in developing any other type of practical software system.

Data as a collaborative hub
> For AI to be data-centric, the *subject-matter experts* who actually understand the data and how to label it must be first-class citizens of the development process alongside data scientists and ML engineers.

Enter weak supervision. Instead of hand-labeling data, researchers have developed techniques that leverage more efficient, programmatic, and sometimes noisier forms of supervision—for example, rules, heuristics, knowledge bases, and more—to create *weakly labeled* datasets upon which high-quality AI models can be rapidly built. These weaker forms of supervision can often be defined programmatically and can often be directly developed by subject-matter experts. AI models that used to need person-years of labeled data can now be built using only person-days of effort and managed programmatically in more transparent and adaptable ways, without impacting performance or quality. Organizations large and small have taken note of this fundamental change in how AI models are built and managed; in fact, in the last hour you have almost certainly used a weakly supervised AI system in your day-to-day life. In the world of data-centric AI, weak supervision has become a foundational tool.

In this context, this book on practical weak supervision could not be more timely. To make use of weak supervision in the real world, practitioners must be exposed to both the core concepts behind weak supervision and the most important software tools in the area. We are honored that the authors have chosen to focus on Snorkel—one of the first and most widely adopted weak supervision software packages, developed by our team at the Stanford AI lab along with contributions from many in the community—as an exemplar for how weak supervision can be made both practical and accessible.

In this book, you will be exposed to the tools necessary to use weak supervision in your own applications. Chapter 1 provides an introduction to weak supervision, and Chapter 2 presents an overview of how the Snorkel software system works. The majority of the book—Chapters 3 to 6—focuses on teaching the reader how to (a) build weakly labeled datasets for real applications in text and vision using Snorkel; (b) leverage those weakly labeled datasets to build state-of-the-art deep learning models with modern software frameworks like Hugging Face Transformers and Torchvision; and (c) apply these techniques with large-scale data. After reading this book, you should be able to recognize when weak supervision would be a good fit for your ML problem and understand how to use the Snorkel software ecosystem to build weakly supervised AI applications.

Importantly, while the open source Snorkel package used in this book is a powerful tool for learning about weak supervision, the state of practical weak supervision is rapidly progressing. Exciting advances in areas like handling sequential data, modeling intricate dependency structures in weak supervision sources, handling nuanced and multipart task types and data modalities, supporting more accessible and efficient interfaces, handling production deployment at scale, and much more can be found in both the recent academic literature as well as in the work of companies like Snorkel AI (*http://www.snorkel.ai*), which is building an advanced commercial platform for data-centric AI (called Snorkel Flow) on top of the foundations of practical weak supervision to which this book introduces the reader.

We at Snorkel are both honored and humbled by the work that the authors have put into showcasing the community's work on this important topic, and we are as excited as ever for the future of data-centric AI.

— Alex Ratner
Cofounder and CEO, Snorkel AI
Palo Alto, CA
September 2021

Preface

Getting quality labeled data for supervised learning is an important step toward training performant machine learning models. In many real-world projects, getting labeled data often takes up a significant amount of time. Weak supervision is emerging as an important catalyst for enabling data science teams to fuse insights from heuristics and crowd-sourcing to produce weakly labeled datasets that can be used as inputs for machine learning and deep learning tasks.

Who Should Read This Book

The primary audience of the book will be professional and citizen data scientists who are already working on machine learning projects and face the typical challenges of getting good-quality labeled data for these projects. They will have working knowledge of the programming language Python and be familiar with machine learning libraries and tools.

Navigating This Book

This book is organized roughly as follows:

- Chapter 1 provides a basic introduction to the field of weak supervision and how data scientists and machine learning engineers can use it as part of the data science process.

- Chapter 2 discusses how to get started with using Snorkel for weak supervision and introduces concepts in using Snorkel for data programming.

- Chapter 3 describes how to use Snorkel for labeling and provides code examples on how one can use Snorkel to label a text and image dataset.

- Chapters 4 and 5 are included as part of the book to enable practitioners to have an end-to-end understanding of how to use a weakly labeled dataset for text and image classification.

- Chapter 6 discusses the practical considerations for using Snorkel with large datasets and how to use Spark clusters to scale labeling.

Conventions Used in This Book

The following typographical conventions are used in this book:

Italic

Indicates new terms, URLs, email addresses, filenames, and file extensions.

`Constant width`

Used for program listings, as well as within paragraphs to refer to program elements such as variable or function names, databases, data types, environment variables, statements, and keywords.

`Constant width bold`

Shows commands or other text that should be typed literally by the user.

`Constant width italic`

Shows text that should be replaced with user-supplied values or by values determined by context.

 This element signifies a tip or suggestion.

 This element signifies a general note.

 This element indicates a warning or caution.

Using Code Examples

All the code in the book is available in the following GitHub repository *https://bit.ly/ WeakSupervisionBook*. The code in the chapters is correct but is a subset of the overall codebase. The code in the chapters is meant to outline the concepts. To run the code for yourself, we encourage you to clone the book GitHub repository.

If you have a technical question or a problem using the code examples, please send email to *bookquestions@oreilly.com*.

This book is here to help you get your job done. In general, if an example code is offered with this book, you may use it in your programs and documentation. You do not need to contact us for permission unless you're reproducing a significant portion of the code. For example, writing a program that uses several chunks of code from this book does not require permission. Selling or distributing examples from O'Reilly books does require permission. Answering a question by citing this book and quoting example code does not require permission. Incorporating a significant amount of example code from this book into your product's documentation does require permission.

We appreciate, but generally do not require, attribution. An attribution usually includes the title, author, publisher, and ISBN. For example: "*Practical Weak Supervision* by Wee Hyong Tok, Amit Bahree, and Senja Filipi (O'Reilly). Copyright 2022 Wee Hyong Tok, Amit Bahree, and Senja Filipi, 978-1-492-07706-0."

If you feel your use of code examples falls outside fair use or the permission given above, feel free to contact us at *permissions@oreilly.com*.

O'Reilly Online Learning

 For more than 40 years, *O'Reilly Media* has provided technology and business training, knowledge, and insight to help companies succeed.

Our unique network of experts and innovators share their knowledge and expertise through books, articles, and our online learning platform. O'Reilly's online learning platform gives you on-demand access to live training courses, in-depth learning paths, interactive coding environments, and a vast collection of text and video from O'Reilly and 200+ other publishers. For more information, visit *http://oreilly.com*.

How to Contact Us

Please address comments and questions concerning this book to the publisher:

O'Reilly Media, Inc.
1005 Gravenstein Highway North
Sebastopol, CA 95472
800-998-9938 (in the United States or Canada)
707-829-0515 (international or local)
707-829-0104 (fax)

We have a web page for this book, where we list errata, examples, and any additional information. You can access this page at *https://oreil.ly/practicalWeakSupervision*.

Email *bookquestions@oreilly.com* to comment or ask technical questions about this book.

For news and information about our books and courses, visit *http://oreilly.com*.

Find us on Facebook: *http://facebook.com/oreilly*

Follow us on Twitter: *http://twitter.com/oreillymedia*

Watch us on YouTube: *http://youtube.com/oreillymedia*

Acknowledgments

The authors will like to thank the following people, who helped us significantly in improving the content and code samples in the book:

- Alex Ratner, Jared Dunnmon, Paroma Varma, Jason Fries, Stephen Bach, Braden Hancock, Fred Sala, and Devang Sachdev from Snorkel for their valuable reviews, suggestions, and pointers. Their input helped us tremendously to improve the book.

- Technical reviewers Siyu Yang, Hong Lu, and Juan Manuel Contreras for their effort and insightful suggestions that helped us improve the content and code samples.

- Jeff Bleiel, Kristen Brown, Rebecca Novack, and the rest of the O'Reilly team for being part of this book-writing journey. From the initial book brainstorms to the countless hours spent on reviewing the books, edits, and discussions, we could not have done it without the amazing support from the O'Reilly team.

Writing a book is a journey and would not have been possible without strong family support; the authors spent many weekends and holidays working on the book. We would like to thank our family for supporting us on this journey.

- I'm thankful for my wife, Meenakshi, for her patience and keeping the coffee on; my daughter Maya for believing in me and correcting my grammar with minimal eye-rolling; our dog Champ for forgiving me, no matter how buggy the code; and finally, to our readers for looking up and taking a leap of faith; may you have as wonderful a journey as I have had creating this—the long nights, the code, the data, the primitive debugging experience! Don't let the logic kill off the magic! —Amit

- I'm grateful for all the inspiration I have had over the years from many friends and coworkers, for Llambi's unconditional love and support, and for the joy and wisdom Ansen and Ennio added to our lives. —Senja

- This is dedicated to the wonderful love in my life—Juliet, Nathaniel, and Jayden. Love for the family is infinite. —Wee Hyong

## CHAPTER 1

Introduction to Weak Supervision

Deep learning is data-hungry. A great amount of data is required for training deep learning models. The growing popularity of deep learning approaches fuels the need for larger, labeled datasets. On the other hand, the trend that we are seeing is that large deep learning models often need more data to work better. Recent key artificial intelligence (AI) achievements would not have been possible without labeled data.

The cost of creating, cleaning, and labeling training data often is a significant expense in terms of both time and money. Furthermore, in some cases, privacy is a key requirement, and an "eyes-off" approach, wherein machine learning practitioners cannot directly inspect the data to provide labels, isn't possible given sensitive and personally identifiable information (PII) in the data.

In this book, you will learn practical techniques that will enable you to leverage weak supervision in your machine learning projects and to address the challenges and high costs of acquiring a high-quality labeled dataset.

Before we do that, let's learn about why weak supervision is important for practical machine learning (ML). In this chapter, we will share practical use cases on how weak supervision can help overcome some of the challenges of implementing ML in the enterprise. We will provide an overview of the different types of weak supervision approaches and introduce Snorkel, a new machine learning framework. Finally, we will cover a new paradigm called data programming, which builds on weak supervision and the benefits it provides.

What Is Weak Supervision?

Weak supervision is a broad collection of techniques in machine learning in which models are trained using sources of information that are easier to provide than hand-labeled data, where this information is incomplete, inexact, or otherwise less accurate.

Instead of a subject-matter expert (SME) hand-labeling high-quality data, all of which is very cost-prohibitive, we can use other techniques that combine diverse sources of data, creating an approximation of labels. Using weak supervision, we can reconcile these labels to a single label.

Weak supervision enables these noisy, weakly sourced labels to be combined programmatically to form the training data that can be used to train a model.

Labels are considered "weak" because they are noisy—i.e., the data measurements that the labels represent are not accurate and have a margin of error. The labels are also considered "weak" if they have additional information that does not directly indicate what we want to predict.

The model created using training data generated via weak supervision is comparable in performance to a supervised learning model created with traditional "strong" labels. In addition, as researchers at the Massachusetts Institute of Technology (MIT)[1] discovered, using a combination of a few "strong" labels along with a larger "weak" label dataset resulted in a model that not only learned well but also trained at a faster rate.

Before we get into the details of weak supervision, let's first look at some real-world use cases.

Real-World Weak Supervision with Snorkel

Snorkel started as a project at Stanford in 2016 with the premise that users can programmatically label, build, and manage training data. The research around Snorkel also pushed innovations on other related tasks, such as data augmentation, multitask learning, and eyes-off training. Snorkel has since expanded and has partnered with companies and research institutes such as DARPA, Google, and Intel.

Building on this research, Snorkel (an open source project) has expanded into a commercial company called Snorkel.ai. The primary product of Snorkel AI is Snorkel Flow (*https://www.snorkel.ai/platform*), a data-centric platform for building AI applications that enterprises can adopt for their AI teams. Snorkel Flow supports a Python SDK and developer APIs, and also has a GUI no-code interface that allows both technical and nontechnical business users to incorporate weak supervision when building applications.

For the scope of this book, where we are learning about the underlying programmatic labeling technology, we will use the open source version of Snorkel and not the commercial platform of Snorkel Flow.

---

1 Joshua Robinson, Stefanie Jegelka, and Suvrit Sra, "Strength from Weakness: Fast Learning Using Weak Supervision" (Preprint, submitted February 19, 2020), *https://arxiv.org/abs/2002.08483*.

Weak supervision and Snorkel help address the MLOps challenges such as model governance, operations, data lineage, etc. Weak supervision expressed as code allows us a lot of flexibility as we incorporate different data points. This helps improve generalization and can easily scale with unlabeled data.

Programmatic Weak Supervision May Help Address Bias

Programmatic weak supervision can be useful in improving explainability and reducing bias. Unlike most ML models, which are opaque-box, in weak supervision, we write the code that generates the training data. As a result, we can have more fine-grained control over how labels are created. As an example, it is possible to observe which labeling functions contribute and how they are being combined when using programmatic weak supervision to train and create an ML model.

This ability to interpret opens up opportunities to identify and address bias in our data or those that might arise during inference when deployed in production.

Snorkel has been used in many real-world applications across industry, medicine, and academia. Industry applications include product classification,[2] bootstrapping conversational agents,[3] and many others. Rapidly identifying new knowledge from the scientific literature is a long-standing challenge in natural language processing (NLP), and Snorkel has been used to build a database of novel genetic associations using scientific documents[4] and mine chemical-disease relations.[5]

In electronic health records (EHRs), patient notes are an important source of information for AI in health care. Snorkel has been used to extract outcome labels for medical imaging[6] and improve radiology report labeling,[7] monitor medical device

2 Stephen H. Bach et al., "Snorkel DryBell: A Case Study in Deploying Weak Supervision at Industrial Scale" (Preprint, submitted June 3, 2019), *https://arxiv.org/abs/1812.00417v2*.

3 Neil Mallinar et al., "Bootstrapping Conversational Agents with Weak Supervision" (Preprint, submitted December 14, 2018), *https://arxiv.org/abs/1812.06176v1*.

4 Volodymyr Kuleshov et al., "A Machine-Compiled Database of Genome-Wide Association Studies," *National Communications* 10, no. 1 (July 2019): 341, *https://doi.org/10.1038/s41467-019-11026-x*.

5 Emily K. Mallory et al., "Extracting Chemical Reactions from Text Using Snorkel," *BMC Bioinformatics* 21, no. 217 (2020): 1–15, *https://link.springer.com/content/pdf/10.1186/s12859-020-03542-1.pdf*.

6 Jared Dunnmon et al., "Cross-Modal Data Programming Enables Rapid Medical Machine Learning Patterns" (Preprint, submitted March 26, 2019), *https://arxiv.org/abs/1903.11101*.

7 Akshay Smit et al., "CheXbert: Combining Automatic Labelers and Expert Annotations for Accurate Radiology Report Labeling Using BERT" (Preprint, submitted October 18, 2020), *https://arxiv.org/abs/2004.09167v3*.

safety,[8] classify risk factors like smoking status,[9] and continuously monitor COVID-19 symptoms[10] supported by medical NER (named-entity recognition).

Let's take a look at some real-world use cases showing how Snorkel allows us to get labeled data more easily and how companies have successfully leveraged this paradigm for their needs.

Industrial image defect detection

Researchers at the Korea Advanced Institute of Science and Technology[11] have used Snorkel as part of a system that creates a dataset of images of defective products. These images are then used for training a computer vision model to recognize defective products in the production line. The team uses a combination of crowdsourcing, data augmentation, and data programming. They start with the SMEs—the workers in the assembly line—and ask them to classify the objects based on the defect patterns.

The images in each category are then augmented with the help of GANs (generative adversarial networks). Images from those categories are analyzed, and the distribution of the pixels for lines across the x- and y-axis is generated. Those distributions are the feature vectors, supplied then to a multilayer perceptron trainer, which will perform training and learn the model. The labeling functions consist of the learned model for each pattern emitting a prediction on whether the image contains the respective defect or not.

Labeling biomedical data for gene clustering

One of the problems bioinformatics deals with is predicting the function of a gene. Often, this is done by studying the proteins that those genes code, which is a process known as gene expression. A protein can be coded by more than one gene; studying gene expression often is treated as a classification problem.[12]

Researchers at the computational bioinformatics Indian Institute of Technology Patna[13] utilized Snorkel to label gene expression data. They initially clustered the

8 Alison Callahan et al., "Medical device surveillance with electronic health records", *npj Digital Medicine* 2, no. 94 (2019), *https://doi.org/10.1038/s41746-019-0168-z*.

9 Yanshan Wang et al., "A Clinical Text Classification Paradigm Using Weak Supervision and Deep Representation," *BMC Medical Informatics and Decision Making* 19, no. 1 (2019), *https://link.springer.com/article/10.1186/s12911-018-0723-6*.

10 Jason Fries et al., "Ontology-Driven Weak Supervision for Clinical Entity Classification in Electronic Health Records," *Nature Communications* 12, no. 2017 (2021), *https://www.nature.com/articles/s41467-021-22328-4*.

11 Geon Heo et al., "Inspector Gadget: A Data Programming-Based Labeling System for Industrial Images" (Preprint, submitted August 21, 2020), *https://arxiv.org/abs/2004.03264*.

12 Pratik Dutta and Sriparna Saha, "A Weak Supervision Technique with a Generative Model for Improved Gene Clustering" (IEEE Congress on Evolutionary Computation, 2019), *https://oreil.ly/zfw8R*.

13 Dutta and Saha, "A Weak Supervision Technique with a Generative Model for Improved Gene Clustering."

data using a multiobjective optimization (MOO) technique, aiming at optimizing three objectives. For MOO, a solution is said to dominate another solution if all its objective values are better than the values of another solution. The nondominated solutions of a MOO are the ones for which there are no solutions for all the objective functions doing better than them. Dutta and Saha used those nondominated solutions from the gene expression clustering as the labels for the data.

Intent classification

This task consisted of detecting and classifying the intent of a user allowing for more intelligent and better experiences for the user—including automatically performing actions based on intent to help answer questions. The input to the labeling functions is user actions and interactions with various systems such as search, emails, and recommendation systems. Many of these interactions can be correlated with the intent of the action by the user; these correlations of action and intent can also be noisy, making weak supervision a great paradigm to implement.

Intel Osprey

Intel and Stanford's researchers built Osprey, a weak supervision system on top of Snorkel specifically designed for highly imbalanced datasets.[14] Osprey is unique as it is an end-to-end ML pipeline that allows nontechnical business users to create labeling functions using a GUI—without writing any code. Osprey supports generalization using a novel ensembling technique and achieving a high precision level by combining a label-based generative model with a discriminative model.

Snorkel DryBell

Researchers from Stanford, Brown, and Google[15] cooperated to create Snorkel DryBell, a weak supervision framework based on Snorkel, utilized to solve labeling data at Google for tasks like:

Topic classification

This task consisted of creating a new classifier to detect the topic in the textual content. The heuristic used in the labeling functions for this data looked at the URL of the datasource—heuristics related to statistics regarding the named-entity recognition (NER) appearing in the content, and heuristics based on the prediction of existing topic models, outputting semantic categorizations for the content.

---

14 Eran Bringer et al., "Osprey: Weak Supervision of Imbalanced Extraction Problems without Code," in *Proceedings of ACM Conference (DEEM)*, (Association for Computing Machinery, Amsterdam, NL, June 2019), *https://ajratner.github.io/assets/papers/Osprey_DEEM.pdf*.

15 Bach et al., "Snorkel DryBell: A Case Study in Deploying Weak Supervision at Industrial Scale."

Product classification

This task needed labeled data in order to build a classifier to detect content references to products in particular categories. The labeling functions looked at the keywords in the content and made use of the Google Knowledge Graph to translate the keywords into another language. Finally, it explored predictions from the semantic topic model to set apart content that was not related to the categories of interest.[16]

Event classification

This task consisted of classifying real-time events into different categories. The weak classifiers used were again model-based: making use of other existing models' predictions, heuristics instead of characteristics of the event, and knowledge-graph-based labeling function to look at the relationship of the events and the entity related to the event.

We will explore Snorkel in more detail in Chapter 2, but first let us understand the different approaches to weak supervision that make up the broader umbrella of weakly supervised learning.

Approaches to Weak Supervision

Weak supervision can be used along with many other types of supervision and can be broken down broadly into three different approaches. The type of information and labels available determine which of these three different approaches would work better for that situation:

- Incomplete supervision
- Inexact supervision
- Inaccurate supervision

Incomplete Supervision

In incomplete supervision, we have a small set of training data that is of high quality and is labeled but is not enough data to train a model; the remaining training data is not labeled. This is quite common.

Say we want to classify news (fake versus authentic). It is relatively straightforward to get news datasets from the internet. However, labeling all of it would be quite a task

---

16 Ekin Dogus Cubuk et al., "AutoAugment: Learning Augmentation Policies from Data" (Preprint, submitted April 11, 2019), *https://arxiv.org/abs/1805.09501*.

because of time and cost. For a small set of this news dataset, a human can label and classify the news; the rest is left as unlabeled and incomplete.

At a high level, we have three approaches for incomplete supervision: active learning, which is with human help; semisupervised learning, in which no person is involved; and transfer learning.

Active learning

This approach is all about a human (typically an SME) in the loop and involves finding strong labels for data by an SME. However, instead of directly querying strong labels for the most informative samples, we first query weak labels and optimize the most important labels allowing an SME to concentrate on only that subset. This output from active learning acts as weak labels and inputs to weak supervision—nicely complementing each other.

When it comes to selecting the most important labels from an unlabeled dataset, there can be many criteria. The two most common ones are informativeness and representativeness.[17] For an unlabeled set of data, informativeness tells us the degree to which uncertainty has been reduced. Representativeness, on the other hand, measures how well that dataset represents the structure of the input patterns.[18]

Semisupervised learning

Unlike active learning, instead of using an SME, the goal is to use assumptions that are task-agnostic and domain-specific, supported by heuristics on the unlabeled data. At a high level, we use a data distribution and clustering approach and outline a belief that similar data has similar characteristics and output. This leads to two basic premises that help in labeling data: cluster assumption and manifold assumption.

Cluster assumption

This is the premise that data has some inherent pattern that allows us to cluster data points, and to these clusters, we can apply some class labels.

Manifold assumption

This is the premise that clusters that are closer (to each other) have similar predictions and lie on a manifold.

---

17 Sheng-Jun Huang, Rong Jin, and Zhi-Hua Zhou, "Active Learning by Querying Informative and Representative Examples," *IEEE Transactions on Pattern Analysis and Machine Intelligence* 36, no. 10 (October 2014, *https://doi.org/10.1109/TPAMI.2014.2307881*.

18 Burr Settles, "Active Learning Literature Survey" in *Computer Sciences Technical Report 1648* (University of Wisconsin–Madison, January 9, 2009), *https://research.cs.wisc.edu/techreports/2009/TR1648.pdf*.

Transfer learning

Here we would use models trained on another dataset and apply them to the data and task we are interested in. The data and its shape would be similar, and we would expect to fine-tune the model for our task. This can also involve combining several tasks to understand relationships from an approximate domain that might not be obvious.

Semisupervised approaches

There are four types of semisupervised approaches:

Generative methods

This assumes both the labeled and unlabeled data is generated from the same model. This allows us to view unlabeled data as missing values and to use techniques such as expectation-maximization algorithms.

Graph-based methods

This uses a graph in which nodes correlate to training instances, and relations (e.g., distance or similarity) between the data points are modeled as edges between different instances. The unlabeled data points can be propagated on this graph.

Low-density separation methods

These are density-based sorting algorithms that try to place classification boundaries across less dense regions between the clusters of the input space.

Disagreement-based methods

Here we have multiple learner instances that collaborate and work on a task. During this process, they might have overlapping and conflicting data points. These conflicts and disagreements are used as the key to learning.

What Are Expectation-Maximization Algorithms?

Expectation-maximization algorithms (EM algorithms) is a general technique that helps in finding the maximum likelihood estimators in latent variable models. Latent variables are *hidden* variables that are not directly visible but are inferred using other (observable) variables.

EM algorithms are widely used in ML algorithms, especially in unsupervised learning settings, such as clustering and density estimation.

Transductive learning

Transductive learning is different than a typical ML approach, which is based on induction where one is *attempting* to discover rules based on the training data, and these rules are induced via a model. We essentially are generalizing rules to apply to a class problem.

On the other hand, in the transductive learning approach, instead of solving a class problem, we solve for that instance problem. We use training data to discover rules, which are then used to make better predictions for the same type of training data—essentially, it being an *instance* problem and not a *class* problem.

Figure 1-1 at a high level outlines the differences between the approaches for incomplete supervision.

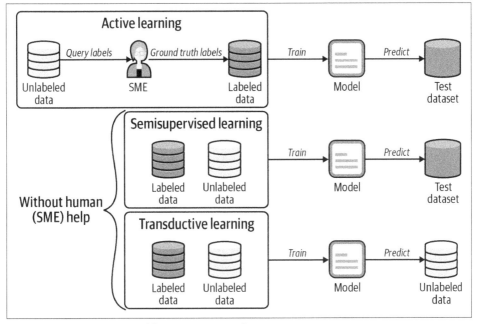

Figure 1-1. Semisupervised learning approaches

Inexact Supervision

In inexact supervision, we have labels and features (i.e., metadata) on the training dataset. The label information is not complete, and the information is the kind we prefer as it relates to the task at hand—hence the name "inexact." In addition, the metadata associated with the training dataset is imprecise, and the labels are poor.

For example, say we need to detect fraudulent activity for a financial organization from a set of transactions. Typically, we do not have details that directly correlate to what we would classify as fraud. However, if we have labeled examples of other types of fraud transactions from other datasets (nonfinancial), we can use these other examples to predict the label for the original set of transactions. Here we don't have the exact labels, and combining additional similar but nonfinancial examples of fraud labels makes this inexact. Inexact supervision uses multi-instance learning.

What Is Multi-Instance Learning?

Multi-instance learning is a type of weakly supervised learning for situations in which we have training examples but have incomplete knowledge about *labels* of those training examples. These training examples are grouped in sets called bags. Within a certain bag, the specific training instances, while different from each other, are still similar. A label is provided for the entire bag but not specific instances within that bag.

There are positive and negative bags. If at least one instance in a bag is positive, that bag is labeled positive. Conversely, if all the instances in a bag are negative, that bag is labeled negative. The goal of multi-instance training is to classify unseen instances and bags using labeled bags as training data.

Multi-instance learnings can be applied to many use cases and domains; some examples are:

- Content-based image retrieval allowing image classification based on their subject
- Molecule classification allowing one to predict if a molecule produces a given effect
- Object localization in an image—allowing one to find specific objects in an image such as medical image diagnosis
- Sentiment analysis in the text

Inaccurate Supervision

As the name suggests, in inaccurate supervision the information has errors, with some of the ground truth labels either not accurate or not high quality. Usually, this happens when one is crowdsourcing data and there are distractions and inaccuracies, or when the data is difficult to categorize. The idea is to band together possibly mislabeled examples and then try to correct them. Think of it as an approximate correction.

One way to correct the labels is to learn from data engineering, in which we use techniques such as neighborhood graph and measure connected nodes within the graph to look for outliers and missing information.

 Data programming and data engineering sound very similar, but they are quite different. Data engineering deals with the science and knowledge of large-scale data flows, data pipelines, data exploration and transformation (ETL) including data cleaning, and preparation. A lot of this is specific to the underlying database implementation and the runtime optimization.

In the next section, we will learn about data programming. This is a technique that is foundational when using Snorkel and helps address the one-off and ad hoc implementations of weak supervision.

Data Programming

Data programming is a new paradigm that allows for the generation of a large set of labeled training datasets programmatically. In data programming, a user creates a set of simple programmable functions called labeling functions that are used to label the data. Each of these labeling functions provides a label for each training example (or it abstains). By running multiple labeling functions, we get useful but potentially conflicting information about the label for each example. Data programming enables us to aggregate these votes into a coherent probability distribution over the true, unknown labels.

Until more recently, weak supervision was being applied in a very isolated and ad hoc manner, and it used a subset of available data. This caused suboptimal performance. Data programming helps standardize this ad hoc nature of weak supervision with a more unified and formal approach. Compared to traditional ML approaches for training data, data programming allows a richer, more flexible, and generic approach.

Recent AI milestones have demonstrated that fundamentally the ML algorithms haven't dramatically evolved; what has changed is the amount of data used. The data is much more (i.e., bigger) and has better, cleaner labels. Today, most ML solutions are trending toward a more comprehensive end-to-end solution, which requires even more labeled data to work. The only way we can scale is with data programming, which helps us create training data programmatically. Being a program, it can be assembled, labeled, and debugged. The code that enables this is called labeling functions; these functions create weak labels that allow us to use weak supervision.

Crowdsourcing Labeling

There are additional ways to scale labeling and leverage human effort for data labeling and cleaning. Crowdsourcing through platforms like Amazon's Mechanical Turk (MTurk) is one example. MTurk allows us to use gig workers for our labeling needs. Compared to using a few SMEs (to label the data), the options with MTurk (see Figure 1-2) are more scalable but still have logistical and practical constraints.

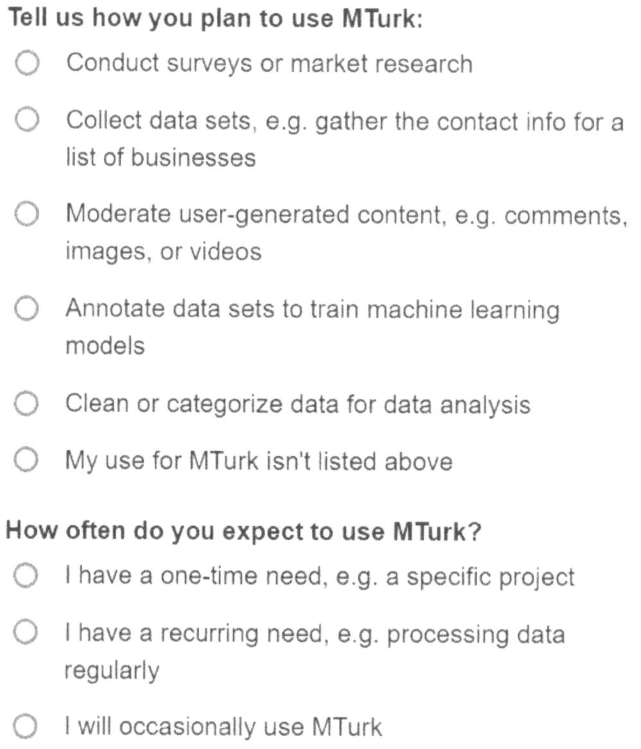

Tell us how you plan to use MTurk:

○ Conduct surveys or market research

○ Collect data sets, e.g. gather the contact info for a list of businesses

○ Moderate user-generated content, e.g. comments, images, or videos

○ Annotate data sets to train machine learning models

○ Clean or categorize data for data analysis

○ My use for MTurk isn't listed above

How often do you expect to use MTurk?

○ I have a one-time need, e.g. a specific project

○ I have a recurring need, e.g. processing data regularly

○ I will occasionally use MTurk

Figure 1-2. Mechanical Turk (MTurk) planned use

Data programming has many advantages. Using data programming, you can:

- Encode domain knowledge representing real-life constraints and situations in reusable and updatable form rather than in individual training labels
- Simultaneously incorporate a wide range of supervision resources for training in a principled way
- Reduce the time and effort required to deploy new models

Data programming helps bring other benefits such as version control, reusability, modularity, maintainability, etc. We will explore more details on data programming in Chapter 2.

Getting Training Data

Weak supervision is an approach that is more efficient and scalable to address the training data gap compared to other techniques. When using weak supervision, we can have diverse inputs that contribute to the training data. These diverse inputs are:

Pattern-based heuristics
Allow an SME to feature annotate and help bootstrap based on specific patterns instead of arbitrary and unknown correlations.

Distant supervision
Allows data points that heuristically align with an external knowledge base to generate noisy labels.

Weak classifiers
Allows for classifiers that are not a good fit (for the task at hand) to be used on a different dataset to create noisy and biased datasets; this becomes the training set.

Labeling function generators
Allows for programmatic weak supervision systems such as Snorkel (which we will explore in Chapter 2) to generate multiple functions using code. Given this programmable code, this makes these generators more scalable and manageable.

All this progress in algorithms is driving the need for larger everything—larger models with more parameters, which require larger training datasets. Instead of picking one set of data sources to get all this large training dataset, weak supervision is the unifying method to get different types and sources of data together (see Figure 1-3)—allowing the scale needed for this progress to continue.

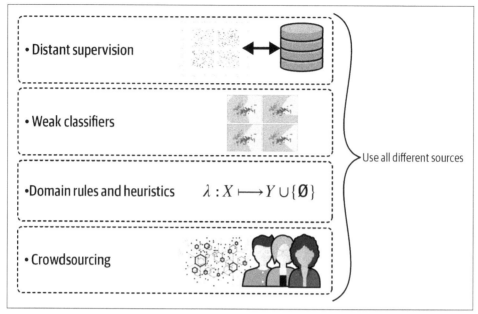

Figure 1-3. Unifying method for weak supervision

How Data Programming Is Helping Accelerate Software 2.0

Instead of "software is eating the world," a new trend—"ML is eating software"—is starting to emerge. There have been a few leading academics[19] and industry leaders[20] who have been highlighting this shift in software development and programming. This new phenomenon is loosely called "Software 2.0" (SW2.0), which is not something far out in the future. It is happening now, and in some production cases, it is already responsible for a 1000x productivity increase.

One example is Google's neural machine translation. The codebase for it went down from 500K lines of C++ code to approximately 500 lines of ML code[21]—a very impressive leap. We are seeing this trend also in classical computer science problems such as database tuning, networks, ETL, and data cleaning, etc. This was possible only because ML replaced swaths of code and heuristics. Software 2.0 is indeed starting to eat Software 1.0.

---

19 Christopher Ré, "Software 2.0: Machine Learning Is Changing Software," (lecture, HAI Weekly Seminar with Chris Ré, January 27, 2021), *https://hai.stanford.edu/events/hai-weekly-seminar-chris-re*.

20 Andrej Karpathy, "Software 2.0," *Medium*, November 11, 2017, *https://karpathy.medium.com/software-2-0-a64152b37c35*.

21 Jack Clark, "Import AI: #63: Google Shrinks Language Translation Code from 500,000 to 500 Lines with AI, Only 25% of Surveyed People Believe Automation=Better Jobs," *Import AI* (blog), October 9, 2017, *https://oreil.ly/6qrCs*.

With SW2.0 we are moving from innovating and reinventing a new ML model to understanding which signals to put in an ML model. This ML model is combining several off-the-shelf SOTA (state-of-the-art) models and is used as part of an application. This is also making the end-to-end process more efficient. This speed is achieved by abstracting to more ML-optimized and efficient hardware compared to generic hardware.

ML is fundamentally changing how we build, deploy, and manage code in production; with SW2.0 we are shifting from conventional programming to high-level domain knowledge that programs using lots of training data. Much of this training data is powered by weak supervision, and Snorkel could be one of the critical pieces required to *program* this SW2.0.

Software 2.0 Architecture

In the SW2.0 architecture, we are not ripping out and replacing the system components with ML implementations. Instead, we are fundamentally changing the system components and what they do, and data programming and its potential to create training data are at the heart of that change.

A typical AI application can be divided into three aspects: a model, data, and some compute hardware for training (see Figure 1-4). Both the model and compute aspects are getting to be commodities, and the one different thing is the training data. Most users would *pip install* a SOTA model instead of hand-cranking a new model.

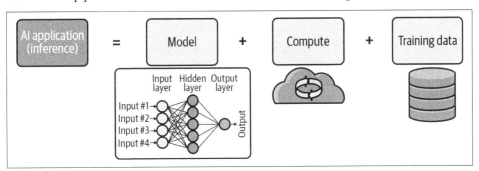

Figure 1-4. Typical AI application

In a world where models are commodities and everything is a data flow, the development time for SW2.0 is greatly reduced compared with "traditional DL." SW2.0 paradigm also has a very interesting side benefit, with the SOTA models doing most of the heavy-lifting allowing enterprises to concentrate time and effort on the long tail of edge cases.

With SW2.0 we are also seeing a cycle, which is creating a flywheel. SW2.0 uses the latest SOTA model and also uses new methods of gathering varied quality training data. Over time, this new training data is used to create the next iteration of the SOTA models. These new generations of SOTA models are then incorporated back into SW2.0—completing the flywheel. Data programming and Snorkel's ability to work across several types of data (text, image, video, time series, real time, etc.) makes Snorkel ideal in the new world of "hands-free" engineering, where we don't hand-tune features or hand-label training data to get high quality.

A Note on the Code

All the code in the book can be cloned from a GitHub repository (*https://bit.ly/WeakSupervisionBook*).

The code that is in the book is meant to help us understand the core concepts and follow along. While the code in the chapters is correct, in the interest of space, we leave out some of the boilerplate code. Trying to copy the code from within the book might cause some of the code not to execute.

We encourage you to clone the book GitHub repository to use.

Summary

Data programming is a new machine learning paradigm for creating and managing training datasets for ML algorithms. Programming is changing, with ML models and techniques much easier to incorporate and use but increasingly more difficult to create.

The appetite for labeled data is going to just keep growing exponentially. To do practical machine learning, the cost and complexity of getting high-quality labeled training data need to be carefully managed. In addition, other issues for practical machine learning include model management, dealing with bias, AI ethics considerations, interpretability of models, and more.

Data programming is emerging as a unifying method for weak supervision, in which one can combine different sources and methods and use them all instead of picking one.

Weak supervision, together with the notion of data programming, presents an exciting approach toward solving part of the problem of getting a high-quality training label. In the next few chapters, we are excited to share with you how you can get started.

## CHAPTER 2

Diving into Data Programming
with Snorkel

Before the advent of deep learning, data scientists would spend most of their time on feature engineering: working to craft features that enabled models to perform better on some metric of choice. Deep learning, with its ability to discover features from data, has freed data scientists from feature engineering and has shifted their efforts toward other tasks like understanding the selected features, hyperparameter tuning, and robustness checks.

With the recent advent of the "deep learning era," data engineering has rapidly become the most expensive task in terms of both time and expense. This task is particularly time-consuming for scenarios in which data is not labeled. Enterprises gather a lot of data, but a good part of that is unlabeled data. Some enterprise scenarios, like advertising, naturally enable gathering raw data and their labels at the same time. To measure whether the advertising presented to the user was a success or not, for instance, a system can log data about the user, the advertisement shown, and whether the user clicked on the link presented, all as one record of the dataset. Associating the user profile with this data record creates a ready-to-use labeled dataset.

However, applications such as email, social media, conversation platforms, etc., produce data that cannot be easily associated with labels at the time the dataset is created. To make this data usable, machine learning practitioners must first label the data—often via processes that are time-consuming—and scale linearly with the size of the unlabeled data.

Tackling the data labeling process is at the heart of weak supervision. In this chapter, we will focus on data programming techniques for weak supervision offered by the Snorkel software package.

Snorkel, a Data Programming Framework

Snorkel is a framework that implements easy-to-use, modern solutions for key data engineering operations like data labeling and data augmentation through a lens called "data programming." For data labeling, practitioners can encode the heuristics they use to classify samples of data to different categories using standard software tools, leverage state-of-the-art statistical modeling techniques to estimate the accuracies of these heuristics, and programmatically create "weakly labeled" data by applying those heuristics to unlabeled data and aggregating their signal using the learned statistical model.

For data augmentation, Snorkel allows data engineers to amplify limited datasets by generating new samples that respect known invariances, ensuring that models trained on the resulting data are able to do the same.

To install Snorkel, simply use pip:

```
pip install snorkel
```

Looking at the contents of the Snorkel package (*https://oreil.ly/hutT3*), you will notice that the main subpackages are:

Labeling
Tools to generate labels for the data, and reconcile those labels generating a single one at the end

Analysis
Utilities to calculate metrics evaluating labeling

Augmentation
Tools that help generate new data samples

Slicing
Tools to monitor how a subset of data with particular characteristics has affected the training

Classification
Tools to train multitask models

In the rest of this chapter, we will dive deeper into how to leverage the labeling, analysis, and augmentation subpackages for our data programming needs. Although we will not cover the "slicing" package, we recommend getting familiar with it. The Snorkel.org site has a really good tutorial on it (*https://oreil.ly/jdain*).

Let's get labeling!

Getting Started with Labeling Functions

In Snorkel, "labeling functions" encode the rules that the data engineers or domain experts follow to assign each sample of data to a particular class. Labeling functions may be written in any number of ways, but the most common is via simple Python snippets.

The best way to get started creating labeling functions is to get to know subsets of data that share properties that provide signals for the problem of interest. You can then proceed to create functions:

- That test each data sample for those properties
- That, for a classification problem (which we'll focus on here), either "vote" to assign the data point to one of the classes or abstain

Intuitively, you can think of each labeling function as a weak classifier that operates over some subset of the data. Typically, you would want to create several labeling functions for any given problem. These labeling functions can be noisy and correlated and use whatever external resources might be useful; the statistical modeling behind Snorkel will do the heavy lifting to aggregate the signal from the labeling functions into weak labels for each data point.

Let's get practical about how to use Snorkel. Suppose we wish to train a classifier that attempts to determine whether integers are prime or not. To train, we need labeled examples: pairs of integers and their corresponding prime/not prime tags. However, we only have an unlabeled set of data. Our goal, with Snorkel, is to create a set of labels by writing labeling functions. Next, we show a set of examples for this scenario:

```
data = [5, 21, 1, 29, 32, 37, 10, 20, 10, 26, 2, 37, 34, 11, 22, 36, 12, 20,
31, 25]
df = pd.DataFrame(data, columns=["Number"])
```

The preceding code creates an array of 20 integers, `data`. It then initializes a Pandas DataFrame with a single column named "Number," and the values of the `data` array as records. Next let's establish our convention of which numeric labels will correspond to the prime numbers and which to the nonprime numbers:

```
ABSTAIN = -1
NON_PRIME = 0
PRIME = 1
```

As you can see, besides the `PRIME` and `NON_PRIME` labels, we have introduced a third option `ABSTAIN`. `ABSTAIN` will be used when none of the rules encoded seems to match the data point that is being analyzed. Note that the `ABSTAIN` option has important (and positive!) implications for the ability of Snorkel's statistical modeling techniques to estimate labeling functions' accuracy.

The next step is to define our "labeling functions." Here, our labeling functions are regular Python functions that contain logic indicating whether:

- A given sample is prime
- An example is not prime
- The status of the example is unclear based on the logic coded by the function (ABSTAIN)

The @labeling_function() decorator (*https://oreil.ly/I8Uqr*) is what makes a given Python function a labeling function in code. The argument passed to the decorator is the dataset row.

For our prime/nonprime labeling problem, one of the labeling functions could encode whether a number is odd or even. If the number is even, the function will vote for this record to not be a prime number. This logic is not complete because the number 2 is even and is prime as well, but it also is the only even prime, and the Snorkel labelers do not need to be perfect; they only need to be better than random chance. Recall further that each labeling function can provide a signal on some subset of the data and abstain for the remainder, allowing other labeling functions to handle the uncovered portion.

First, let's import the package containing the definition of the labeling function decorators:

```
from snorkel.labeling import labeling_function
```

Next, let's code the is_even labeling function, as we just described it:

```
@labeling_function()
def is_even(record):
    if record["Number"] % 2 == 0:
        return NON_PRIME
    else:
        return ABSTAIN
```

Another labeling function can be is_odd. As the name suggests, this function can check whether the number is odd and, if not, suggest that it is not a prime number.

> The logic of the is_even function is identical to the logic of the is_odd function, and we should not use two identical functions in practice. Those two functions are used here just to illustrate that Snorkels can successfully deal with highly correlated labeling functions.

The logic for the is_odd function would be:

```
@labeling_function()
def is_odd(record):
    if record["Number"] % 2 == 1:
        return ABSTAIN
    else:
        return NON_PRIME
```

Another labeling function can be one that "knows" that number 2 is a prime number, as illustrated in this sample:

```
@labeling_function()
def is_two(record):
    if record["Number"] == 2:
        return PRIME
    else:
        return ABSTAIN
```

The final labeling function we will use encodes "knowing" that some specific numbers are prime, and it only votes for those ones to be PRIME, abstaining for all other numbers. Let's call this function is_known_prime:

```
#The list of "known" prime numbers
known_primes = [2, 3, 5, 7, 11, 13, 17, 19, 23, 29]

@labeling_function()
def is_known_prime(record):
    if record["Number"] in known_primes:
        return PRIME
    else:
        return ABSTAIN
```

Now that we have our labeling functions, we will proceed to use them on the dataset.

Applying the Labels to the Datasets

The process of getting the labeling functions to "vote" on each record is called "applying the labeling functions." The family of objects that applies the labeling functions is called appliers. There are several appliers:

DaskLFApplier
    Applies the defined labeling functions to the Dask DataFrames (*https://oreil.ly/ IGnFn*) (Dask is a DataFrame composed of smaller Pandas DataFrames that are accessed and operated upon in parallel).

PandasLFApplier
    Applies the array of labeling functions to a Pandas DataFrame.

`PandasParallelLFApplier`

> This applier operates by parallelizing the Pandas DataFrame into a Dask Data-Frame and uses the `DaskLFApplier` to work on the partitions in parallel, being therefore faster than the `PandasLFApplier`.

`SparkLFApplier`

> Applies the labeling functions over a Spark Resilient Distributed Dataset (RDD).

For our example, since the data is small and the process can easily run on a desktop or laptop, we will be using the `PandasLFApplier`.

Let's import the Snorkel `PandasLFApplier`:

```
from snorkel.labeling import PandasLFApplier
```

Next, let's define an array, `lfs`, where we will declare all the labeling functions, followed by the applier `PandasLFApplier`. The `applier.apply` call applies the labeling functions to the DataFrame `df`:

```
lfs = [
        is_odd,
        is_even,
        is_two,
        is_known_prime
      ]

applier = PandasLFApplier(lfs=lfs)
L_train = applier.apply(df=df)
```

Analyzing the Labeling Performance

After applying the labeling functions, we can run an analysis on how they are performing. Snorkel comes equipped with `LFAnalysis`, which summarizes the performance of the labeling functions by describing polarity, coverage, overlaps, and conflicts. To make use of `LFAnalysis`, let's start with importing the package and then print the `LFAnalysis` summary:

```
from snorkel.labeling import LFAnalysis

LFAnalysis(L=L_train, lfs=lfs).lf_summary()
```

The output is a Pandas DataFrame, summarizing these four metrics (see Table 2-1).

Table 2-1. The `LFAnalysis.lf_summary()` DataFrame

Number	j	Polarity	Coverage	Overlaps	Conflicts
is_odd	0	[0]	0.55	0.55	0.05
is_even	1	[0]	0.55	0.55	0.05
is_two	2	[1]	0.05	0.05	0.05
is_known_prime	3	[1]	0.20	0.05	0.05

Polarity

Polarity shows which labels each labeling function has emitted when evaluated over a given set of data (note that ABSTAIN is not considered a label). Polarity is therefore 0 for is_odd and is_even, because those functions are built to either ABSTAIN or return NON_PRIME (we defined NON_PRIME = 0), while for is_two and is_known_prime polarity is 1, because those two functions are built to either ABSTAIN or return PRIME (PRIME = 1).

When would looking at the polarity come in particularly handy? Imagine we had a labeling function that was expected to return both classes—e.g., 0 and 1—but the observed polarity is only 0. This could indicate an error in the logic that returns class 0, so we should check for any potential bugs. If there are no bugs, it might also be worth double-checking our reasoning around that logic, as we are not obtaining the expected empirical results.

The polarity itself can also be retrieved through the `lf_polarities()` call:

```
LFAnalysis(L=L_train, lfs=lfs).lf_polarities()

[[0], [0], [1], [1]]
```

Coverage

For each labeling function, the coverage metric indicates what fraction of the data the labeling function did not abstain for and returned one of the other values (Table 2-2). In other words, coverage is a measure of how often your labeling functions have opinions about examples in the datasets.

Table 2-2. The coverage metric for the `LFAnalysis` DataFrame

	Coverage
is_odd	0.55
is_even	0.55
is_two	0.05
is_known_prime	0.20

To understand the values presented by coverage, we can apply each labeling function to the DataFrame and inspect the results:

```
df["is_odd"] = df.apply(is_odd, axis=1)
df["is_even"] = df.apply(is_even, axis=1)
df["is_two"] = df.apply(is_two, axis=1)
df["is_known_prime"] = df.apply(is_known_prime, axis=1)
```

The output will be in the DataFrame in Table 2-3.

Table 2-3. The DataFrame with the results of the labeling functions applied to each record

Number	is_odd	is_even	is_two	is_known_prime
5	−1	−1	−1	1
21	−1	−1	−1	−1
1	−1	−1	−1	−1
29	−1	−1	−1	1
32	0	0	−1	−1
37	−1	−1	−1	−1
10	0	0	−1	−1
20	0	0	−1	−1
10	0	0	−1	−1
26	0	0	−1	−1
2	0	0	1	1
37	−1	−1	−1	−1
34	0	0	−1	−1
11	−1	−1	−1	1
22	0	0	−1	−1
36	0	0	−1	−1
12	0	0	−1	−1
20	0	0	−1	−1
31	−1	−1	−1	−1
25	−1	−1	−1	−1

If we look at one of the labeling functions, is_odd, for example, has returned a value different from ABSTAIN (NON_PRIME) for 11 out of 20 records, as we can see in Table 2-4. That is why the coverage for this labeling function is 11/20 or 0.55.

Table 2-4. The subset of data for which is_odd has returned a nonABSTAIN value

Number	is_odd	is_even	is_two	is_known_prime
32	0	0	−1	−1
10	0	0	−1	−1
20	0	0	−1	−1
10	0	0	−1	−1
26	0	0	−1	−1
2	0	0	1	1
34	0	0	−1	−1
22	0	0	−1	−1
36	0	0	−1	−1
12	0	0	−1	−1
20	0	0	−1	−1

The coverage can also be retrieved through the `lf_coverages()` call:

```
LFAnalysis(L=L_train, lfs=lfs).lf_coverages()
array([0.55, 0.55, 0.05, 0.2 ])
```

The coverage of the labeling functions should match your expectations about the distribution of the characteristics used by each labeling function in your validation data. If you encode a rule thinking that it should not abstain for 30% of the data, and you see it covering 90% of the data, it is time to check the logic of the labeling function or examine your expectations.

Overlaps

The overlaps metric is a measure of how often two labeling functions vote on the same points. Concretely, it indicates what fraction of the data nonABSTAIN return values from one labeling function have overlapped with nonABSTAIN return values from another labeling function. Practically, as you can see above in Table 2-4, the `is_known_prime` function has returned a PRIME value 4 out of 20 times: for numbers 5, 29, 2, and 11. It has ABSTAIN-ed for all other records.

As we can see in Table 2-5, for those same four records, only in the case of number 2 have the other labeling functions emitted a *0* or a *1*. `is_known_prime` has overlapped only once with another labeling function, 1/20; therefore, its measure is 1/20 or 0.05.

Table 2-5. The DataFrame with the labeling functions applied

Number	is_odd	is_even	is_two	is_known_prime
5	−1	−1	−1	1
29	−1	−1	−1	1
2	0	0	1	1
11	−1	−1	−1	1

The calculations are the same for the other labeling functions. If we look at Table 2-6, the is_odd and is_even both overlap with each other or the other two functions 11/20 times or 0.55.

Table 2-6. The LFAnalysis.lf_summary() *DataFrame*

Number	Overlaps
is_odd	0.55
is_even	0.55
is_two	0.05
is_known_prime	0.05

The overlaps can also be calculated through the lf_overlaps() call:

```
LFAnalysis(L=L_train, lfs=lfs).lf_overlaps()
array([0.55, 0.55, 0.05, 0.05])
```

Conflicts

Conflicts indicate the fraction of the data in which this labeling function's nonabstaining decision has conflicted with another labeling function's nonabstaining decision.

We can see in Table 2-7 that for each labeling function, that ratio seems to be 0.05 or 1/20 samples. Inspecting the DataFrame presented in Table 2-3, where we put together the output of each labeling function in a column, we can see that there is a single record that has some disagreement between all labeling functions, as you can see in Table 2-8. This record is behind the 0.05 conflicts statistics.

Table 2-7. The `LFAnalysis.lf_conflicts()` *DataFrame*

	Conflicts
is_odd	0.05
is_even	0.05
is_two	0.05
is_known_prime	0.05

Table 2-8. The DataFrame with the labeling functions applied

Number	is_odd	is_even	is_two	is_known_prime
2	0	0	1	1

Labeling functions that conflict significantly with other labeling functions may be useful so long as they are not worse than random chance; otherwise, they might need a more careful look.

The conflicts can also be calculated through the `lf_conflicts()` call:

```
LFAnalysis(L=L_train, lfs=lfs).lf_conflicts()

array([0.05, 0.05, 0.05, 0.05])
```

Using a Validation Set

Let's assume that for a small portion of the data, we have ground truth labels. This data can serve as a validation set. Even when we do not have a validation set, it often is possible to label a subset of the data using subject-matter experts (SMEs). Having this validation dataset (10%–20% the size of the training data, depending on how representative of the entire dataset you think that portion is) can help evaluate further the labelers. On this set, we can calculate the additional statistics: "Correct," "Incorrect," and "Empirical Accuracy."

To make use of the validation set, we would start by applying the labeling functions to it:

```
# define a validation set, and create a DataFrame
validation = [22, 11, 7, 2, 32]
df_val = pd.DataFrame(validation, columns=["Number"])

# gather the ground truth labels
true_labels = np.array([0, 1, 1, 1, 0])

# apply the labels
L_valid = applier.apply(df_val)
```

```
# analyze the labelers and get the summary df
LFAnalysis(L_valid, lfs).lf_summary(true_labels)
```

The resulting DataFrame will have the additional three-column statistics from the initial one presented in Table 2-9: Correct, Incorrect, and Empirical Accuracy.

Table 2-9. The LFAnalysis.lf_summary() DataFrame for the validation set

	j	Polarity	Coverage	Overlaps	Conflicts	Correct	Incorrect	Emp. Acc.
is_odd	0	[0]	0.6	0.6	0.2	2	1	0.666667
is_even	1	[0]	0.6	0.6	0.2	2	1	0.666667
is_two	2	[1]	0.2	0.2	0.2	1	0	1.000000
is_known_prime	3	[1]	0.6	0.2	0.2	3	0	1.000000

The Correct and Incorrect statistics are the actual count of samples this labeling function has correctly or incorrectly labeled. It is easier to interpret these numbers by looking at the output of the labeling functions. Doing this, of course, is just for this illustration, as it does not scale in practice:

```
df_val = pd.DataFrame(validation, columns=["Number"])
df_val["is_odd"] = df_val.apply(is_odd, axis=1)
df_val["is_even"] = df_val.apply(is_even, axis=1)
df_val["is_two"] = df_val.apply(is_two, axis=1)
df_val["is_known_prime"] = df_val.apply(is_known_prime, axis=1)
df_val
```

"Empirical Accuracy" is the percentage of samples that have been labeled correctly, ignoring samples in which the labeling function abstained. Looking at Table 2-10, we can see that the is_known_prime labeling function has returned PRIME for three samples, and they have all been correct; therefore, its Empirical Accuracy is 1.0. The is_even function, on the other hand, has been correct for 2/3 nonABSTAIN returns; therefore, its accuracy is 67%.

Table 2-10. The df_val DataFrame

Number	is_odd	is_even	is_two	is_known_prime	ground_truth
22	0	0	−1	−1	0
11	−1	−1	−1	1	1
7	−1	−1	−1	1	1
2	0	0	1	1	1
32	0	0	−1	−1	0

Reaching Labeling Consensus with LabelModel

After creating the labeling functions and making use of the statistics to check on our assumptions and debug them, it is time to apply them to the dataset. In the process, for each record, we will get several "opinions," one from each labeling function (unless one is abstaining), regarding which class a given example should belong to. Some of those class assignments might be conflicting, and therefore we need a way to resolve the conflicts in order to assign a final label. To reach this single-label conclusion, Snorkel provides the LabelModel class.

The LabelModel learns a model over the predictions generated by the labeling functions using advanced unsupervised statistical modeling, and uses the predictions from this model to assign a probabilistic weak label to each data point. To infer values for new datapoints, initially a LabelModel gets "fit" to the data, and then the data points to generate predictions that are passed to the predict method of this Label-Model. You can see the results for some select data points in Table 2-11.

```
label_model = LabelModel()
label_model.fit(L_train=L_train, n_epochs=200, seed=100)
preds_train_label = label_model.predict(L=L_train)
preds_valid_label = label_model.predict(L=L_valid)
L_valid = applier.apply(df_val)
LFAnalysis(L_valid, lfs).lf_summary()

preds_train_labelingModel = label_model.predict(L=L_train)
preds_valid_labelingModel = label_model.predict(L=L_valid)

df["preds_labelingModel"] = preds_train_labelingModel
```

Table 2-11. The DataFrame records for a few selected entries, including the predictions from the LabelModel

Number	preds_labelingModel	is_odd	is_even	is_two	is_known_prime
5	1	-1	-1	-1	1
21	-1	-1	-1	-1	-1
32	0	0	0	-1	-1
2	0	0	0	1	1

The LabelModel estimates the accuracy of each labeling function given the particular labeling function's predictions and how they relate to the output of all other labeling functions. Those estimates are used as the parameters of the LabelModel, which learns to predict a single label. The relationship between the labeling functions and the latent true label is modeled as a graphical model, shown in Figure 2-1. The Label-Model class estimates the parameters of this graphical model each time it is fit.

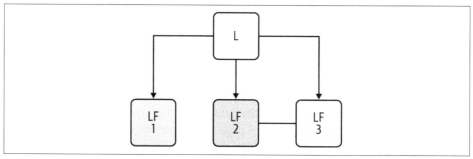

Figure 2-1. The labeling functions graphical model

Intuition Behind LabelModel

The agreement and disagreement of the labeling functions serve as the source of information to calculate the accuracies of the labeling functions. The `LabelModel` combines these agreements and disagreements with a type of independence—conditional independence—to obtain certain relationships that enable solving for the accuracies. The intuition behind why this is possible relates to the fact that if we have enough labeling functions, even just examining the most popular vote will provide a noisy, but higher-quality, estimate of the true label. Once this has been obtained, we can examine how each labeling function performs against this label to get an estimate of its accuracy. The actual functionality of the `LabelModel` avoids this two-step approach and instead uses an application of the law of total probability and Bayes' rule. Given conditional independence of the labeling functions *S1*, *S2*, it holds that

$$P(S1,S2) = P(S1, S2, Y=-1) + P(S1, S2, Y=+1) +$$

$$= P(S1, S2 \mid Y=-1)P(Y=-1) + P(S1, S2 \mid Y=+1)P(Y=+1) +$$

$$= P(S1 \mid Y=-1)P(S2 \mid Y=-1)P(Y=-1) + P(S1 \mid Y=+1)P(S2 \mid Y=+1)P(Y=+1)$$

The lefthand side contains the agreement/disagreement rate between the two labeling functions, while the last equation contains the sum of products of accuracies (and the priors $P(Y)$).

Now we can obtain at least two more such equations by adding additional labeling functions. We can then solve for the accuracy terms such as $P(S1 \mid Y=-1)$, either via gradient descent or by solving a system of equations.

LabelModel Parameter Estimation

Earlier we provided some of the intuition behind how Snorkel obtains the accuracy parameters from agreements and disagreements among a few labeling functions. This can be generalized into an algorithm to obtain all of the accuracies. There are several

Reaching Labeling Consensus with LabelModel

After creating the labeling functions and making use of the statistics to check on our assumptions and debug them, it is time to apply them to the dataset. In the process, for each record, we will get several "opinions," one from each labeling function (unless one is abstaining), regarding which class a given example should belong to. Some of those class assignments might be conflicting, and therefore we need a way to resolve the conflicts in order to assign a final label. To reach this single-label conclusion, Snorkel provides the `LabelModel` class.

The LabelModel learns a model over the predictions generated by the labeling functions using advanced unsupervised statistical modeling, and uses the predictions from this model to assign a probabilistic weak label to each data point. To infer values for new datapoints, initially a LabelModel gets "fit" to the data, and then the data points to generate predictions that are passed to the `predict` method of this Label-Model. You can see the results for some select data points in Table 2-11.

```
label_model = LabelModel()
label_model.fit(L_train=L_train, n_epochs=200, seed=100)
preds_train_label = label_model.predict(L=L_train)
preds_valid_label = label_model.predict(L=L_valid)
L_valid = applier.apply(df_val)
LFAnalysis(L_valid, lfs).lf_summary()

preds_train_labelingModel = label_model.predict(L=L_train)
preds_valid_labelingModel = label_model.predict(L=L_valid)

df["preds_labelingModel"] = preds_train_labelingModel
```

Table 2-11. The DataFrame records for a few selected entries, including the predictions from the `LabelModel`

Number	preds_labelingModel	is_odd	is_even	is_two	is_known_prime
5	1	−1	−1	−1	1
21	−1	−1	−1	−1	−1
32	0	0	0	−1	−1
2	0	0	0	1	1

The LabelModel estimates the accuracy of each labeling function given the particular labeling function's predictions and how they relate to the output of all other labeling functions. Those estimates are used as the parameters of the LabelModel, which learns to predict a single label. The relationship between the labeling functions and the latent true label is modeled as a graphical model, shown in Figure 2-1. The Label-Model class estimates the parameters of this graphical model each time it is fit.

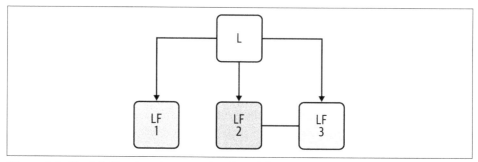

Figure 2-1. The labeling functions graphical model

Intuition Behind LabelModel

The agreement and disagreement of the labeling functions serve as the source of information to calculate the accuracies of the labeling functions. The `LabelModel` combines these agreements and disagreements with a type of independence—conditional independence—to obtain certain relationships that enable solving for the accuracies. The intuition behind why this is possible relates to the fact that if we have enough labeling functions, even just examining the most popular vote will provide a noisy, but higher-quality, estimate of the true label. Once this has been obtained, we can examine how each labeling function performs against this label to get an estimate of its accuracy. The actual functionality of the `LabelModel` avoids this two-step approach and instead uses an application of the law of total probability and Bayes' rule. Given conditional independence of the labeling functions $S1, S2$, it holds that

$$P(S1,S2) = P(S1, S2,Y{=}{-}1) + P(S1, S2,Y{=}{+}1) +$$

$$= P(S1, S2 \mid Y{=}{-}1)P(Y{=}{-}1) + P(S1, S2 \mid Y{=}{+}1)P(Y{=}{+}1) +$$

$$= P(S1 \mid Y{=}{-}1)P(S2 \mid Y{=}{-}1)P(Y{=}{-}1) + P(S1 \mid Y{=}{+}1)P(S2 \mid Y{=}{+}1)P(Y{=}{+}1)$$

The lefthand side contains the agreement/disagreement rate between the two labeling functions, while the last equation contains the sum of products of accuracies (and the priors $P(Y)$).

Now we can obtain at least two more such equations by adding additional labeling functions. We can then solve for the accuracy terms such as $P(S1 \mid Y{=}{-}1)$, either via gradient descent or by solving a system of equations.

LabelModel Parameter Estimation

Earlier we provided some of the intuition behind how Snorkel obtains the accuracy parameters from agreements and disagreements among a few labeling functions. This can be generalized into an algorithm to obtain all of the accuracies. There are several such algorithms; the one used in Snorkel is described in more depth in an article by Ratner et al.[1]

As we saw, the key requirement was having conditional independence between labeling functions. A useful tool to represent the presence of such independences is a graphical model. These are graphical representations of dependence relationships between the variables, which can be used to obtain valid equations with the form previously described. Remarkably, the graph structure also relates to the inverse of the covariance matrix between the labeling functions and the latent label node, and this relationship enables a matrix-based approach to solving for the accuracy parameters.

Specifically, it is possible to complete the inverse of the covariance matrix just based on the agreement and disagreement rates between the labeling functions. Having done this, we have access to the accuracies—the off-diagonal blocks of this covariance matrix—and can then better synthesize the labeling function votes into probabilistic labels using the graphical model formulation.[2]

To illustrate the intuition about learning the probability of the accuracy of each labeling function with an example based on agreement/disagreement, let's imagine that we want to solve the following classification problem: separating a set of images into indoor and outdoor categories. Let's also assume that we have three labeling functions recognizing features related to the sky, clouds, and wooden floor. The labeling function describing the sky features and the labeling function describing the clouds will probably agree in most pictures on whether the picture is indoor or outdoor, and have the opposite prediction with a labeling function judging whether or not there is a wooden floor in the picture. For data points, we will have a DataFrame like the one represented in Table 2-12.

Table 2-12. Example DataFrame for an indoor/outdoor image classification problem

image	has_sky	has_clouds	has_wooden_floor
indoor0	0	0	1
indoor1	0	0	1
indoor2	0	0	1
outdoor3	1	1	0
outdoor4	1	1	0
outdoor5	0	1	0

1 Alexander Ratner et al., "Training Complex Models with Multi-Task Weak Supervision" (Preprint, submitted December 7, 2018), *https://arxiv.org/pdf/1810.02840*.

2 Paroma Varma et al., "Learning Dependency Structures for Weak Supervision Models," *Proceedings of the 36th International Conference on Machine Learning* 97 (June 2019): 6418-6427. *https://arxiv.org/abs/1903.05844*.

To train a LabelModel on this DataFrame, we would do the following:

```
L = np.array(df[["has_sky", "has_clouds", "has_wooden_floor"]])
label_model = LabelModel()
label_model.fit(L)
np.round(label_model.get_weights(), 2)
```

When you examine the weights of the label_model for each classification source (labeling function), you will notice how the first labeling function, has_sky, is weighted less than the second one, has_clouds, due to the mistake it makes on data point "outdoors5":

```
array([0.83, 0.99, 0.01])
```

The calculated conditional probabilities for each source and each class (outdoor, indoor, abstain) are retrieved in the following way:

```
np.round(label_model.get_conditional_probs(), 2)
```

And the actual conditional probability values placed in a matrix with dimensions [*number of labeling function, number of labels* + 1(for abstain), *number of classes*], rounded are as follows:

```
array([[[0.  , 0.  ],
        [0.66, 0.01],
        [0.34, 0.99]],

       [[0.  , 0.  ],
        [0.99, 0.01],
        [0.01, 0.99]],

       [[0.  , 0.  ],
        [0.01, 0.99],
        [0.99, 0.01]]])
```

Strategies to Improve the Labeling Functions

The "Interactive Programmatic Labeling for Weak Supervision" (*https://oreil.ly/6cAUo*) published at KDD 2019, contains various suggestions on how to iteratively improve the labeling functions. One such suggestion is to focus on the data points where most of the labeling functions abstain or conflict, and look for potential additional patterns. These suggestions are called the "abstain-based" and "disagreement-based" strategies. If you have identified a series of high-accuracy labeling functions, the next step would be to attempt to maximize the coverage from those labelers. If instead you are dealing with low-accuracy labeling functions, the focus should be instead on how the ties are broken.

A more focused strategy suggested in the same paper partitions the data based on patterns observed in it, and attempts to create labeling functions that should return an abstain value for the samples in the partition they are designed for, abstaining otherwise. Indicators of the quality of each labeling function are:

- Having a high fraction of data in the partition for which the labeling function returns one of the classes, referred in this paper as the IF (the inside partition fire rate)

- Having a low OF (outside partition fire rate), meaning the labeling functions return a nonabstain value in the partitions other than the ones they were designed for

- Having an overall low FF (false fire rate), which is the case when the labeling functions return the wrong class

Data Augmentation with Snorkel Transformers

To this point in the chapter, we have focused on how to take advantage of Snorkel data programming techniques to label data using a combination of unlabeled data, human domain expertise encoded in heuristics, and unsupervised statistical modeling. We will now discuss how another set of techniques in Snorkel can be used to further increase the effective size of datasets for machine learning. Specifically, in addition to labeling existing data, we can synthetically generate training data by combining existing data points with transformations to which the task should be invariant. As an example, in computer vision problems, some well-known transformations include rotation, occlusion, brightness variation, etc. This approach to increasing the effective size of a dataset is referred to as "data augmentation."

For text datasets, various methods like the ones presented from Wei and Zou in their 2019 paper "EDA: Easy Data Augmentation Techniques for Boosting Performance on Text Classification Tasks"[3] can effectively increase the dataset size. Their suggestions include: replacing words with their synonyms, inserting random words (like adjectives) without breaking the meaning of the sentence, swapping words, and deleting words to create additional examples. Yu et al.[4] take another approach to the same problem, and augment the text by translating the original samples from English to French and then back to English. Kobayashi[5] uses a predictive bidirectional language model to create new samples by predicting which words would come next after a given snippet.

---

3 Jason Wei and Kai Zou, "EDA: Easy Data Augmentation Techniques for Boosting Performance on Text Classification Tasks" (Preprint, submitted August 25, 2019), *https://arxiv.org/abs/1901.11196*.

4 Adams Wei Yu et al., "QANet: Combining Local Convolution with Global Self-Attention for Reading Comprehension" (Preprint, submitted April 23, 2018), *https://arxiv.org/abs/1804.09541v1*.

5 Sosuke Kobayashi, "Contextual Augmentation: Data Augmentation by Words with Paradigmatic Relations" (Preprint, submitted May 16, 2018), *https://arxiv.org/abs/1805.06201*.

The Snorkel framework has a dedicated package for data augmentation, the Snorkel.augmentation package (*https://oreil.ly/1nQDc*).[6] Similar to how the labeling subpackage uses `labeling functions`, the transformation functions used by the augmentation subpackage work by applying a predefined function to each data point.[7] As a result, for each data point, we obtain a new data point.

The transformation functions get applied through the `@transformation_function()` decorator, similar syntax to the `@labeling_function()`.

For example, if we had a dataset of products and prices, we could create a new data point by replacing the price of an existing product in the dataset with a price that fluctuates 10% from the original one. The transformation function to achieve this would look like the following (assuming the DataFrame has a column named Price):

```
@transformation_function()
def replace(x):
    no = x["Price"]
    if isinstance(no, int):
        ten_percent = int(no/10)
        rand = no
        while(rand == no):
            rand = random.randint(no-ten_percent, no+ten_percent)
            return x["Price"] = rand
    return x["Price"] = -1
```

The function takes the number located in the Price column for this record, calculates its 10%, then generates a number in the [–10%, +10%] range. The function returns a data point with the Price column set to –1 if it is not possible to generate a distinct price, so those records can be easily identified and filtered out. Note that the transformation functions operate on deep copy of the record to avoid modifying the original data point.

For text datasets, Wei and Zou illustrate in their "Easy Data Augmentation" set of techniques[8] that replacing a word with its synonym, inserting, deleting, or swapping words randomly in the sentence will yield new, valid, and useful data points. Let's assume we have a dataset about book reviews, like the Multi-Domain Sentiment Dataset (version 2.0) (*https://oreil.ly/hW0BM*), and the task we want to accomplish is:

---

6 Alexander J. Ratner et al. "Snorkel: Fast Training Set Generation for Information Extraction," *SIGMOD '17: Proceedings of the 2017 ACM International Conference on Management of Data* (2017): 1683–1686, *https://dawn.cs.stanford.edu//pubs/snorkeldemo-sigmod2017.pdf*.

7 Alexander Ratner et al., "Learning to Compose Domain-Specific Transformations for Data Augmentation" (Preprint, submitted Sept 6, 2017), *https://arxiv.org/abs/1709.01643*.

8 Wei and Zou, "EDA: Easy Data Augmentation Techniques for Boosting Performance on Text Classification Tasks."

for every book, we want to build a recommender system based on the analysis of the reviews.

If we decide that we do not have enough data points, we can rely on techniques like the ones in the EDA collection and use the Snorkel `transformation_functions` to create additional reviews that are similar to the originals but not identical. Other successful text augmentation techniques include translating the text from the original language to a different language and then back to the original language, as described by Yu et al.,[9] or predicting the next series of words using a text prediction pretrained model, a technique described by Kobayashi.[10]

Before getting to the specifics of each augmentation technique, let's read the dataset file (*https://nijianmo.github.io/amazon/index.htm*) and create a DataFrame. This dataset is in an XML format. To use the transformation functions, we will need to read the dataset using an XML parser like `xml.etree.ElementTree` and, knowing the schema of the dataset, iterate over all the nodes and extract the text for the DataFrame records:

```python
import xml.etree.ElementTree as et

xtree = et.parse("book.unlabeled")
xroot = xtree.getroot()

df_cols = ["product_name", "review_text"]
records = []

for node in xroot:
    text = node.find("review_text").text.replace('\n', '')
    title = node.find("product_name").text.replace('\n', '')
    records.append({"review_text": text, "product_name": title})

df = pd.DataFrame(records, columns = df_cols)
df.head(4)
```

We preserve only the `product_name` and `review_text` columns, for illustration. Table 2-13 shows a preview of a few records of the dataset.

---

9 Yu et al., "QANet: Combining Local Convolution with Global Self-Attention for Reading Comprehension."

10 Kobayashi, "Contextual Augmentation: Data Augmentation by Words with Paradigmatic Relations."

Table 2-13. The df DataFrame preview, for product reviews

product_name	review_text
Child of God: Books: Cormac Mccarthy	McCarthy's writing and portrayal of
Child of God: Books: Cormac Mccarthy	I was initiated into the world of
Child of God: Books: Cormac Mccarthy	I cannot speak to the literary points
Child of God: Books: Cormac Mccarthy	There is no denying the strain of

Next, let's get to each augmentation technique and the respective `transforma
tion_function`.

Data Augmentation Through Word Removal

To put into action one of the EDA techniques, let's try building a transformation function that will remove all the adverbs from the text. The meaning of the sentence should still be preserved since the adverbs enhance the meaning of the sentence, but their absence still conveys most of the information and leaves the sentence still sounding grammatically correct. We will make use of the NLTK package (*https://oreil.ly/RbPPY*) to tokenize the text and tag the parts of speech (POS) so we can identify and then remove the adverbs.

The NLTK package annotates the adverbs with RB, RBR, and RBS, as shown in Table 2-14.

Table 2-14. NLTK adverb tags

RB	adverb
RBR	adverb, comparative
RBS	adverb, superlative

The `remove_adverbs` function does just what we previously described: tokenizes the sentence, extracts the (word, POS tag) array of tuples, and filters out the elements where the POS is in the `tags_to_remove` list before rejoining the remaining words into a sentence. To leave the sentence grammatically correct, at the end we correct the spacing that might be introduced in front of the period by joining. Decorating the function with `transformation_function` converts this Python function into a Snorkel `transformation_function` that can be easily applied to all elements in the dataset using Snorkel tooling:

```
import nltk
nltk.download("averaged_perceptron_tagger")

tags_to_remove = ["RB", "RBR", "RBS"]
@transformation_function()
```

```
def remove_adverbs(x):
    tokens = nltk.word_tokenize(x["review_text"])
    pos_tags = nltk.pos_tag(tokens)
    new_text = " ".join([x[0] for x in pos_tags if x[1]
        not in tags_to_remove]).replace(" .", ".")
    if(len(new_text) != len(tokens)):
        x["review_text"] = new_text
    else:
        x["review_text"] = "DUPLICATE"
    return x
```

The last several lines of the `remove_adverbs` function checks whether the generated text is any different from the original. By setting the `review_text` to DUPLICATE in this case, we can filter out those records later.

Let's now inspect the outcome of applying this `transformation_function` to one of the reviews:

```
review = "Honest Illusions: Books: Nora Roberts"

df[df.product_name == review].iloc[0]["review_text"]
```

The original review is as follows:

> I simply adore this book and it's what made me go out to buy every other Nora Roberts novel. It just amazes me about the chemistry between Luke and Roxanne. Everytime I read it I can't get over the excitement and the smile it brings to me as they barb back and forth. It's just an amazing story over the course of growing up together and how it all develops. Roxanne is smart and sassy and Luke is just too cool. This romantic duo shines and no one else compares to them yet for me. My very favorite romance.

And the version obtained from the `transformation_function`:

> I adore this book and it's what made me go out to buy every other Nora Roberts novel. It amazes me the chemistry between Luke and Roxanne. Everytime I read it I ca get over the excitement and the smile it brings to me as they barb and forth. It's an amazing story over the course of growing up and how it all develops. Roxanne is smart and sassy and Luke is cool. This romantic duo shines and no one compares to them for me. My favorite romance

Note that the adverbs "simply," "just," "very," "too," and "yet" are missing from the output of the `transformation_function`.

Snorkel Preprocessors

Before passing data to the `labeling_function` or `transformation_function`, Snorkel preprocesses data through dedicated modules. The results of this preprocessing are added to the data points as additional columns that can be accessed from the body of both `labeling_functions` and `transformation_functions`.

One of the built-in Snorkel preprocessors is the `SpacyPreprocessor` (*https://oreil.ly/ BWJac*). The `SpacyPreprocessor` makes use of the spaCy (*https://spacy.io*) NLP package to tokenize the words of the text and attach information about entities, part of speech tags found on the specified text column of a data point.

This is offered for convenience, so the package users don't have to code from scratch (as we did previously for adverbs), tokenizing the text inside the body of the `trans formation_function`, as we did before, but can make use of the output of spaCy by just specifying the `pre` parameter in the `transformation_function` annotation. Using the `SpacyPreprocessor`, the spaCy doc is present and ready for inspection.

Let's first import the `SpacyPreprocessor` module and instantiate it:

```
from Snorkel.preprocess.nlp import SpacyPreprocessor

spacy = SpacyPreprocessor(
    text_field="review_text",
    doc_field="doc",
    language="en")
```

The name of the dataset column containing the text to be processed gets passed to the `text_field` argument and the name of the column where the preprocessing output will be placed is defined in the `doc_field` entry. The third argument is the language of the text. Our `transformation_function` that makes use of the `SpacyPreprocessor` would then be as follows:

```
@transformation_function(pre=[spacy])
def spacy_remove_adverbs(x):
    words_no_adverbs = [token for i, token in enumerate(x.doc)
                        if token.pos_ != "ADV"]
    new_sentence = " ".join([x.text for x in words_no_adverbs])
    if(len(words_no_adverbs) != len(x["review_text"])):
        x["review_text"] = new_sentence.replace(" . ", ". ")
    else:
        x["review_text"]= "DUPLICATE"
    return x
```

The list of Token objects is already present in the doc field. Like the `remove_adverbs` function, the `spacy_remove_adverbs` inspects the part-of-speech tags and removes the ones marked as "AVD" (adverbs) but with much less work!

Data Augmentation Through GPT-2 Prediction

In "Contextual Augmentation: Data Augmentation by Words with Paradigmatic Relations,"[11] Kobayashi proposes text data augmentation by replacing words in the text using a bidirectional language model. As an example of this, we can leverage Snorkel to generate new records of data using predictive language models like GPT-2 (at the time of writing, GPT-2 is the best available open source model for text prediction). There are several versions of the GPT-2 models that can be downloaded from the OpenAI Azure storage account: 124M, 355M, 774M, and 1558M. The models are named after the number of parameters they use.

Let's get started by installing the required packages and downloading one of the models, 355M (so we can strike a balance between accuracy and ease of use), following the instructions in *Developers.md* (*https://oreil.ly/aTSPs*):

```
# Create a Python 3.7 environment
conda create -n GPT2 Python=3.7
# Activate the environment
conda activate GPT2
# Download GPT2
git clone https://github.com/openai/gpt-2.git

pip install -r requirements.txt
pip install tensorflow-gpu==1.12.0 fire regex
# Download one of the pretrained models.
Python download_model.py 355M
```

Now that we have the GPT-2 model, inference scripts, and utilities to encode the text, we can use them to write a Snorkel `transformation_function` that takes as arguments 10 words from the review text and predicts another few words based on it. The core of the Snorkel transformer function is simply invoking a slightly modified version of the `interact_model` method from the GPT-2 repository (*https://oreil.ly/Oub6H*):

```
import fire
import json
import os
import numpy as np
import tensorflow as tf
import model
import sample
import encoder
from Snorkel.augmentation import transformation_function

def interact_model(
    raw_text,
```

---

11 Kobayashi, "Contextual Augmentation: Data Augmentation by Words with Paradigmatic Relations."

```python
        model_name="355M",
        seed=None,
        nsamples=1,
        batch_size=1,
        length= None,
        temperature=1,
        top_k=40,
        top_p=1,
        models_dir=r"C:\gpt-2\models",
    ):
        enc = encoder.get_encoder(model_name, models_dir)
        hparams = model.default_hparams()
        with open(os.path.join(models_dir, model_name, "hparams.json")) as f:
            hparams.override_from_dict(json.load(f))

        if length is None:
            length = hparams.n_ctx // 2

        with tf.Session(graph=tf.Graph()) as sess:
            context = tf.placeholder(tf.int32, [batch_size, None])
            np.random.seed(seed)
            tf.set_random_seed(seed)
            output = sample.sample_sequence(
                hparams=hparams, length=length,
                context=context,
                batch_size=batch_size,
                temperature=temperature, top_k=top_k, top_p=top_p
            )

            saver = tf.train.Saver()
            ckpt = tf.train.latest_checkpoint(os.path.join(models_dir, model_name))
            saver.restore(sess, ckpt)

            context_tokens = enc.encode(raw_text)
            all_text = []
            for _ in range(nsamples // batch_size):
                out = sess.run(output, feed_dict={
                    context: [context_tokens for _ in range(batch_size)]
                })[:, len(context_tokens):]
                for i in range(batch_size):
                    text = enc.decode(out[i])
                    all_text.append(text)
            return ''.join(all_text)

@transformation_function()
def predict_next(x):
    review = x["review_text"]
    # extract the first sentence
    period_index = review.find('.')
    first_sentence = review[:period_index+1]
    #predict and get full sentences only.
    predicted = interact_model(review, length=50)
```

```
last_period = predicted.rfind('.')
sentence = first_sentence+" "+predicted[:last_period+1]
x["review_text"] = sentence
return x
```

The `interact_model` function takes as arguments the initial text, in the `raw_text` argument, as well as a model name and a series of parameters to tune the prediction. It encodes the text, creates a TensorFlow session, and starts generating the sample text.

Let's check one of the examples of prediction using the following record with the review text:

```
df[df.product_name == "Honest Illusions: Books: Nora Roberts"]["review_text"]
.to_list()[0]
```

I simply adore this book and it's what made me go out to buy every other Nora Roberts novel. It just amazes me the chemistry between Luke and Roxanne. Every time I read it I can't get over the excitement and the smile it brings to me as they barb back and forth. It's just an amazing story over the course of growing up together and how it all develops. Roxanne is smart and sassy and Luke is just too cool. This romantic duo shines and no one else compares to them yet for me. My very favorite romance.

Trying the transformation function for this particular entry generates the following text (on different runs, the results will be different. If you need reproducible results, set the seed parameter in `interact_model`):

```
review_txt = "Honest Illusions: Books: Nora Roberts"

predict_next(df[df.product_name == review_txt].iloc[0])
```

This is the output:

I simply adore this book and it's what made me go out to pick up books on it and give them a try. It's a beautiful blend of romance and science, and it's both very simple and complex at the same time. It's something I'd recommend to anyone.

The previous example is generated setting the prediction length to 50, for illustration. For most practical text augmentation tasks—to follow the recommendation of Kobayashi and only generate a word—this parameter should be set to a much smaller value:

```
predicted = interact_model(review, length=5)
```

Data Augmentation Through Translation

As we mentioned in the introduction to this augmentation section, translating text from one language to another, and back to the original language, is an effective augmentation technique, introduced by Yu et al.[12]

Let's get started writing the next `transformation_function` using the Azure Translator (*https://oreil.ly/AXSVN*) to translate text from English to French and back to English. At the moment of this writing, you can deploy a free SKU of the Translator and translate up to two million characters per month.

To deploy the Translator, you can look for the product in Azure Marketplace, as shown in Figure 2-2.

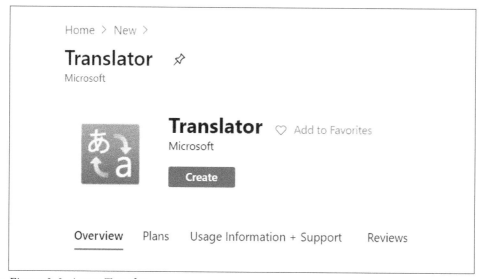

Figure 2-2. Azure Translator

After the deployment, you will need the resource key, the endpoint, and the region of the resource to authenticate the calls to the service. You can find them in the "Keys and Endpoint" view, as shown in Figure 2-3.

---

12 Yu et al., "QANet: Combining Local Convolution with Global Self-Attention for Reading Comprehension."

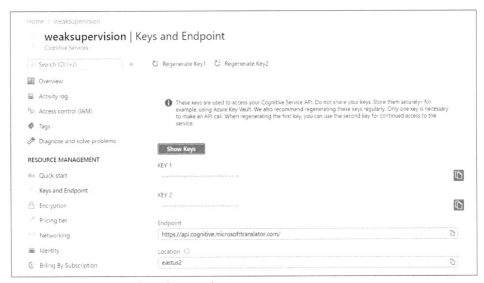

Figure 2-3. Azure Translator keys, endpoint, region

The transformation function request to translate the text is adapted from the GitHub Translator examples (*https://oreil.ly/PdX2r*):

```python
import os, requests, uuid, json
import spacy
nlp = spacy.load("en")

resource_key = "<RESOURCE_SUBSCRIPTION_KEY>"
endpoint = "<ENDPOINT>"
region = "<REGION>"

def translate(text, language):
    headers = {
    "Ocp-Apim-Subscription-Key": resource_key,
    "Ocp-Apim-Subscription-Region" : region,
    "Content-type": "application/json",
    "X-ClientTraceId": str(uuid.uuid4())
    }

    body = [{"text" : text}]
    body = [{"text" : text}]
    response = requests.post(
        endpoint+"/translate?api-version=3.0&to="+language,
        headers=headers, json=body)
    translation = response.json()[0]["translations"][0]["text"]
    print(translation)
    return translation


@transformation_function()
```

```
def augment_by_translation(x):
    text = x["review_text"]
    french = translate(text, "fr")
    english = translate(french, "en")
    score = nlp(text).similarity(nlp(english))
    if(score < 1.0):
        x["review_text"] = english
    else:
        x["review_text"] = "DUPLICATE"
    return x
```

The `translate` function takes the text to translate and the language as arguments, and returns the translated text. The `augment_by_translation` transformation function invokes the `translate` function twice: to translate into French then back to English. The similarity of the original text and the translation is calculated through spaCy's `similarity` routine, which measures the cosine similarity between context-sensitive blocks of text (for the small models). Perfect duplicates would generate a score of 1.0.

Reusing the same example, the review for "Honest Illusions," we can compare the initial English text with the text obtained after retranslating the French output back to English.

English: "I simply adore this book and it's what made me go out to buy every other Nora Roberts novel. It just amazes me the chemistry between Luke and Roxanne. Every time I read it I can't get over the excitement and the smile it brings to me as they barb back and forth. It's just an amazing story over the course of growing up together and how it all develops. Roxanne is smart and sassy and Luke is just too cool. This romantic duo shines and no one else compares to them yet for me. My very favorite romance."

French: "J'adore ce livre et c'est ce qui m'a fait sortir pour acheter tous les autres romans de Nora Roberts. Ça m'étonne la chimie entre Luke et Roxanne. Chaque fois que je le lis, je ca obtenir sur l'excitation et le sourire qu'il m'apporte comme ils barbe et en avant. C'est une histoire incroyable au cours de sa croissance et comment tout se développe. Roxanne est intelligente et impersy et Luke est cool. Ce duo romantique brille et personne ne se compare à eux pour moi. Ma romance préférée."

Back to English: "I love this book and that's what made me come out to buy all the other novels of Nora Roberts. I'm surprised at the chemistry between Luke and Roxanne. Every time I read it, I can get on the excitement and smile it brings me as they beard and forward. It's an incredible story during its growth and how everything develops. Roxanne is smart and impersy and Luke is cool. This romantic duo shines and no one compares to them for me. My favorite romance."

Applying the Transformation Functions to the Dataset

We now have the transformation functions. To be able to use them, we also need to decide upon a policy to use for applying each transformation function to the dataset in order to get a diverse but realistic output. The Snorkel augmentation package contains several policies for this purpose:

ApplyAllPolicy

This policy will take each data point—"book review" in our case—and apply all the transformation functions available to it, one by one, in the same order the `transformation_functions` are listed. The resulting text will be the product of having removed the adverbs, translated, and then supplied to GPT-2 for the next sentence prediction:

```
from Snorkel.augmentation import *

tfs = [predict_next, augment_by_translation, spacy_remove_adverbs]
policy = ApplyAllPolicy(len(tfs), n_per_original=1, keep_original=True)

tf_applier = PandasTFApplier(tfs, policy)
policy.generate_for_example()
```

The `policy.generate_for_example` object contains the list of the indices of the transformation functions selected to be applied to one particular data point, selected at random. The number of new data points to generate for each sample is defined by the `n_per_original` argument. For our case, that would be all of them in order:

```
[[], [0, 1, 2]]
```

This policy will add one more data point per sample, doubling the dataset.

ApplyEachPolicy

Unlike `ApplyAllPolicy`, this policy will apply each `transformation_function` to each data point, separately, without combining them. `keep_original` indicates whether to keep the original data points in the augmented dataset:

```
policy =ApplyEachPolicy(len(tfs), keep_original=True)
policy.generate_for_example()
```

```
[[], [0], [1], [2]]
```

After applying this policy, for each data point, we will have three separate, new data points, each generated from one of the transformation functions.

ApplyOnePolicy

Applies a single policy, the first one, to the data:

```
policy = ApplyOnePolicy(4, keep_original=True)
policy.generate_for_example()
```

```
[[], [0], [0], [0], [0]]
```

After applying this policy, for each dataset record, we will have an additional four records, generated using the first transformation functon from the list (the transformation function at index 0).

RandomPolicy

Creates a list of `transformation_functions` by sampling the list of `tfs` at random. The length of this list is determined by the `sequence_length` argument:

```
policy =RandomPolicy(len(tfs),
    sequence_length=5,
    n_per_original = 2,
    keep_original=True)
policy.generate_for_example()
```

```
[[], [1, 2, 1, 2, 2], [2, 1, 2, 0, 1]]
```

MeanFieldPolicy

This policy is probably the one that will have more uses because it allows the frequency of transformation function application to be defined by a user-supplied probability distribution. With this policy, a sequence of transformations will be applied to each data point, and the order/composition of that sequence will be determined by sampling from the list of transformation functions according to the supplied probability distribution:

```
policy = MeanFieldPolicy(
    len(tfs),
    sequence_length=1,
    n_per_original=1,
    keep_original=True,
    p=[0.3, 0.3, 0.4],
)
policy.generate_for_example()
```

```
[[], [0]]
```

After selecting a policy—for our case, we kept the `MeanFieldPolicy`—we go ahead and apply the policy to the dataset and get the synthetic data points:

```
df_train_augmented = tf_applier.apply(df2)
```

A preview of some of the records of the augmented dataset is shown in Table 2-15.

Table 2-15. The df DataFrame preview, for product reviews

review_text	reviewer
I simply adore this book and it's what made me...	"Book Junkie"
I love this book and that's what made me come ...	"Book Junkie"
I love this book and that's what made me come ...	"Book Junkie"
Magic, mystery, romance and burglary are all p...	"Terry"
Magic , mystery , romance and burglary are all...	"Terry"
Magic , mystery , romance and burglary are all...	"Terry"
I read the review and got the book and fell in...	Diana
I read the review and got the book and fell in...	Diana
I read the review and got the book and fell in...	Diana
It is difficult to find books in this genre th...	A. Rowley
It is difficult to find books in this genre th...	A. Rowley
It's hard to find books like this that have a ...	A. Rowley
This is one of my favorite Nora Roberts book. ...	avid reader "A reader"
It's one of my favorite Nora Roberts books. ."...	avid reader "A reader"
It 's one of my favorite Nora Roberts books	avid reader "A reader"
This book has everything....Love, Greed, Murde...	S. Williams
This book has it all. One thing I really lik...	S. Williams
This book has everything. Some characters we...	S. Williams
When I began to read Nora Roberts, I really di...	Creekergirl
I began to read Nora Roberts , I did n't expec...	Creekergirl
I began to read Nora Roberts , I did n't expec...	Creekergirl

We can now use this dataset to train supervised models.

Summary

Data programming is a promising way to label data. The labeling functions or heuristics are learned on some sample data, and they are then applied to the entire dataset. A `LabelModel` is then trained over the weak labels generated and used to reconcile those weak labels into a final label.

Snorkel has a good solution for data augmentation as well, allowing practitioners to use several augmentation techniques at once or select from a range of techniques controlling in what percentage each technique contributes to the added records.

In the next chapter, we will make use of Snorkel to practically label two datasets: one image and one text.

Labeling in Action

The previous chapter introduced labeling functions decorators. Those decorators convert the Python functions into weak classifiers for the Snorkel framework. In this chapter, we will use those labeling functions to create labeling strategies and label one text dataset and one image dataset.

As mentioned in previous chapters, weak supervision and data programming are all about bringing together information from different sources and extracting information about various shapes of data. To label the text dataset, we will generate fake/real labels out of activities like the following:

- Inspecting particular images embedded in article review websites, indicating through their color (red, green, yellow) the level of veracity of the article they are reviewing

- Summarizing online articles reviewing the news, and extracting their sentiment about the article

- Aggregating agreement among crowdsourced decision-making

As we have one or more of the preceding signals for each article, we will use Snorkel to reach an agreement among those signals.

For the images dataset, we will put together labeling functions that cast their vote on whether the image is an outdoor or indoor scenery by running small image classifiers over the data. These classifiers aim at recognizing elements like the sky, the grass, etc., as well as image recognition techniques to describe the images. We will follow using text classifiers to generate a second opinion about whether each respective image is taken indoors or outdoors. We will again use Snorkel to decide among all those weak labels what best describes the image: an "outdoor" or "indoor" label.

Labeling a Text Dataset: Identifying Fake News

In this section, our goal will be to label whether a particular news article is real or not. The first step would be to create or identify a dataset—a collection of news articles—to work with.

The FNID dataset is one of the datasets present in the IEEE DataPort portal (*https://ieee-dataport.org*). It is created by Fariba Sadeghi, Amir Jalaly Bidgoly, and Hossein Amirkhani,[1] who are members of the University of Qom. The dataset contains two parts: one set of train/validation/test files that follow the structure of the FakeNewsNet (*https://oreil.ly/HYI41*), and the second set of files that follow the structure of the LIAR dataset (*https://oreil.ly/cp5qz*). We are going to work on "fake news detection (FakeNewsNet)" using the Snorkel labeling functions, described in "Getting Started with Labeling Functions" on page 19, to label *fnn-train.csv* of "fake news detection(FakeNewsNet)."[2] Both "fake news detection(FakeNewsNet)" and "fake news detection(LIAR)" are labeled datasets, and therefore our file *fnn_train.csv* is labeled as well, but we are not going to use the labels during our labeling process. We will set aside 20% of the dataset as a validation set and use the original labels to compute the accuracy of the Snorkel `LabelingModel` on this validation set.

The original FakeNewsNet dataset was created to enable the research community to understand the characteristics of real and fabricated news articles. FakeNewsNet is built and labeled using FakeNewsTracker (*https://oreil.ly/fijRY*),[3] a sophisticated system that crawls sites like PolitiFact and BuzzFeed to gather claims and then searches for engagement on those claims in social media and other news sites.

The original FakeNewsNet contains:

News content
   The actual text of the news article

Social context
   The author of the post

Spatiotemporal information
   The publisher of the news

---

1 Fariba Sadeghi, Amir Jalaly Bidgoly, and Hossein Amirkhani, "FNID: Fake News Inference Dataset," IEEE DataPort, August 18, 2020, *https://ieee-dataport.org/open-access/fnid-fake-news-inference-dataset*.

2 Kai Shu et al., "FakeNewsNet: A Data Repository with News Content, Social Context and Spatialtemporal Information for Studying Fake News on Social Media" (Preprint, submitted March 27, 2019), *https://arxiv.org/abs/1809.01286*.

3 Kai Shu et al. "FakeNewsTracker: a tool for fake news collection, detection, and visualization," *Computational and Mathematical Organization Theory* 25 (2019): 60–71. *https://doi.org/10.1007/s10588-018-09280-3*.

Through their paper describing FakeNewsTracker and the process of creating the dataset, Shu, Mahudeswaran, and Liu mention the following methodologies:

- Analyzing the public profiles of the authors
- Analyzing the frequency with which the publishers publish fake or real news
- Analyzing the social network signals like retweets, likes, and crowdsourcing[4]

In this section, our work is based on some of their methodologies, as described in their paper "FakeNewsNet: A Data Repository with News Content, Social Context and Spatialtemporal Information for Studying Fake News on Social Media." In addition, we inquire about several sources that analyze fake news, get more than one "opinion," and use Snorkel's `LabelModel` to aggregate all the votes and produce a single label.

Exploring the Fake News Detection(FakeNewsNet) Dataset

The fake news detection(FakeNewsNet) dataset contains three files: train, validation, and test. We are only using the training file *fnn_train*. This file contains 15212 training samples. The two classes for the records of this data are "real" and "fake."

The columns of the dataset, as seen in Table 3-1, are:

id
    The identifier for each sample, representing the PolitiFact website ID for this article

date
    The time of publishing

speaker
    The person or organization to whom this statement is attributed

statement
    The claim published by the speaker

sources
    The sources that have been used to analyze each statement

paragraph_based_content
    Paragraph from where the statement is taken

---

4 Shu et al., "FakeNewsNet: A Data Repository with News Content, Social Context and Spatialtemporal Information for Studying Fake News on Social Media."

Table 3-1. Preview of the fake news detection(FakeNewsNet) dataset

id	date	speaker	statement	sources	paragraph_based_content	label_fnn
3106	2011-01-25	Joe Wilkinson	A national organization says Georgia has one o…	['http://www.ajc.com/news/georgia-politics-ele…	['A coalition of government watchdog groups la…	fake
5655	2012-04-02	Rick Scott	Says Barack Obama's health care law "will be t…	['http://www.youtube.com/watch?v=TaC0mKApf9Q&f…	['As Supreme Court justices embarked on three …	fake
3506	2011-04-01	J.D. Alexander	Says the Southwest Florida Water Management Di…	['http://www.tampabay.com/news/politics/gubern…	["Here's a new one: The Senate budget committe…	fake

Importing Snorkel and Setting Up Representative Constants

Before diving into our sources of information and labeling strategies, let's import the Snorkel packages that we know we'll need and define variables for our label classes:

```
from snorkel.labeling import labeling_function
from snorkel.labeling import PandasLFApplier
from snorkel.labeling import LFAnalysis
from snorkel.labeling.model import LabelModel
```

As we mentioned in the previous chapter, the classifiers must have the option to abstain. We will assign the number –1 to ABSTAIN, the return value for when no conclusion can be derived. We'll assign the integer 1 to REAL news, and the value 0 to fake news represented by FAKE:

```
ABSTAIN = -1
FAKE = 0
REAL = 1
```

Let's now see how to go about labeling our data.

Fact-Checking Sites

Some of the fact-checking sites that appear in the list of sources are:

- *www.politifact.com*
- *www.snopes.com*
- *www.factcheck.org*
- *factcheck.afp.com*
- *www.washingtonpost.com/news/fact-checker*

- *www.realclearpolitics.com*
- *www.glennbeck.com*

Those sites contain information about the claim and can each serve as a weak signal. The information is represented in each site differently. The first step toward using the information on the site would be to read the content of the site.

We can make use of the `urllib` package utilities to read the content of the site and the `BeautifulSoup` Python package to parse the content of the site:

```
from urllib.request import Request, urlopen
from bs4 import BeautifulSoup
import json

# contacts a url, downloads the website's content and parses it.
def get_parsed_html(url):
    req = Request(url, headers={"User-Agent": "Mozilla/5.0"})
    webpage = urlopen(req).read()
    parsed_html = BeautifulSoup(webpage)
    return parsed_html
```

Let's now look at how to uniquely leverage each one of those sources, starting with PolitiFact.

PolitiFact rating

PolitiFact (*https://www.politifact.com*) is part of the nonprofit Poynter Institute for Media Studies (*https://www.poynter.org*), and it dates back to 2007. The PolitiFact team is composed of journalists, reporters, and editors who either receive claims via email or select significant claims appearing in news outlets and work on checking facts surrounding the statement. The way PolitiFact quantifies the truthfulness to the news is by assigning a Truth-O-Meter rating. There are six ratings in Truth-O-Meter, in decreasing level of truthfulness:

TRUE
  This statement is true.

MOSTLY TRUE
  This statement is accurate but needs additional clarification.

HALF TRUE
  This statement is only partially accurate.

MOSTLY FALSE
  The statement ignores facts that might create a different impression.

FALSE
  The statement is mostly inaccurate.

PANTS ON FIRE

The statement is inaccurate.

PolitiFact uses three editors to research the claim, its source, the material that the source has to back up its claim, etc. At the end of this process, the three editors vote on the status of the claim, generating the Truth-O-Meter rating. An example of the Truth-O-Meter rating is shown in Figure 3-1.

Figure 3-1. Structure of the PolitiFact site commenting on statements; retrieved from https://oreil.ly/wuITa

The PolitiFact site displays the statement as the head of the page, together with an image representing the Truth-O-Meter rating. To extract what this image is for all the PolitiFact URLs in our sources, we inspect the parsed HTML of each site and extract the alt (narrator text) for each one of the Truth-O-Meter images. The alt text corresponds to one of the Truth-O-Meter ratings: true, mostly true, half true, mostly false, false, pants on fire:

```
def get_poitifact_image_alt(url):
    result = "abstain"
    try:
        parsed_html = get_parsed_html(url)
        div = parsed_html.body.find("div", attrs={"class":"m-statement__meter"})
        result = div.find("img",
        attrs={"class":"c-image__original"})["alt"]
    except Exception as e:
        print(e)
    return result
```

As previously mentioned, some samples have more than one PolitiFact URL in their sources. The labeling_function aggregates the signal from all of them, assigning a numeric value to the Truth-O-Meter rating in decreasing value from true to pants-fire.

The dataset contains an additional rating, barely-true, which is not present in the current PolitiFact Truth-O-Meter ratings. This additional rating was added to the truth_o_meter dictionary, containing the string rating to number encoding, used in our labeling function:

```
truth_o_meter = {
    "true": 4,
    "mostly-true": 3,
    "half-true": 2,
    "barely-true": 1,
    "mostly-false": -1,
    "false": -2,
    "pants-fire": -3
}
@labeling_function()
def label_politifact(row):
    total_score = 0
    labels = str(row["www.politifact.com"])
    if labels:
        labels = labels.split(',')
        for label in labels:
            if(label in truth_o_meter):
                total_score += truth_o_meter[label]
    if total_score > 0:
        return REAL
    if total_score < 0:
        return FAKE

    return ABSTAIN
```

For every PolitiFact source rating, the label_politifact function presented will sum up the encoding of each rating and return REAL if the sum is positive, FAKE if it is negative, and ABSTAIN if the rating values cancel each other out.

Given that each sample often has more than one rating, a more accurate labeling function would have taken into account the degree of semantic similarity between the statement in the sample and the statement in the PolitiFact article and assigned a weight to the rating. That weight could have been factored into the total_score calculation.

Snopes rating

Snopes.com (*https://oreil.ly/abuVD*) has been active since early 2000, fact-checking claims and publishing the sources it used to do the fact-checking as well. Their process consists of researching the facts behind the statement, starting with asking additional clarifying questions to the source that published the statement. They further consult experts with established expertise in the field to get their viewpoint and pointers for additional information. Snopes.com strives to use information from peer-reviewed journals and government agencies to check the claim.

Statement example:

```
source: "Bloggers"
statement: "Says Elizabeth Warren, asked about the Mollie Tibbetts murder,
said 'I know this is hard for her family, but they have to remember that we
need to focus on real problems, like illegal immigrants not being able to see
their kids.'"
sources: [... ,
  'https://www.snopes.com/fact-check/elizabeth-warren-mollie-tibbetts/']
```

The visual representation that snopes.com uses to mark the claims is the image in the `media rating` class. Our approach, similar to the PolitiFact site inspection, makes use of the alt text of this rating image. The alt text corresponds to the Snopes ratings, as shown in Figure 3-2.

Claim

Elizabeth Warren trivialized the killing of Mollie Tibbetts (the suspect is an undocumented immigrant) by saying, "We need to focus on real problems" like immigrant family separation.

Rating

Mostly False

About this rating ⬀

Figure 3-2. Snopes rating for the article at https://oreil.ly/wTmYl

The `get_snopes_image_alt` function searches for the image representing the rating, the red triangle in our example in Figure 3-2, and extracts the alt text (text used by screen readers when they go over images) from the image HTML element. The alt text corresponds to snopes.com ratings.

```python
def get_snopes_image_alt(url):
    result = "abstain"
    try:
        parsed_html = get_parsed_html(url)
        div = parsed_html.body.find("div", attrs={"class":"media rating"})
        result = div.find("img")["alt"]
```

```
        except Exception as e:
            print(e)
    return result
```

Some of the snopes.com ratings include the following:

True
> A statement that can be proven true.

Mostly True
> The primary statement is accurate.

Mixture
> This statement is only partially accurate.

Mostly False
> The primary statement can be proven false.

False
> The statement is mostly inaccurate.

Other ratings are "Unproven," "Outdated," "Miscaptioned," "Correct Attribution," etc. For the labeling function, we are returning REAL for the True and Mostly True cases, we abstain for the Mixture case, and we return Fake for all the other ratings. The Correct Attribution rating only indicates that the claim is attributed to the right person but does not have information about the truthfulness of the claim itself, as you can judge from Figure 3-3. Since most controversial claim attributions seem to be around nontrue statements, we are erring on the "this might be fake news" side. ABSTAIN would be another good choice:

```
@labeling_function()
def label_snopes(row):
    label = str(row["www.snopes.com"])
    if label != "nan":
        if "True" in label:
            return REAL
        elif "Mixture" in label:
            return ABSTAIN
        else:
            return FAKE
    else:
        return ABSTAIN
```

Figure 3-3. Example of a probably false claim rated with Correct Attribution; retrieved from https://oreil.ly/BITG5

FactCheck.Org and AFP Fact Check

FactCheck.org (*https://oreil.ly/0kKKO*) is a project of the Annenberg Public Policy Center, which focuses on the claims made by political figures: the president, administration officials, senate, congressional, and party leaders. They select the material to review from the major news outlets as well as the social media profile of these politicians and their official press releases, websites, and political campaigns.

The process by which FactCheck.org does their fact research involves contacting the issuer of the statement to ask about their sources, following with conducting their own independent research on the matter. They aim at using government institutions like the Library of Congress, the Bureau of Labor Statistics, etc., as sources of data to investigate the claims.

AFP (Alliance of the French Press) Fact Check (*https://oreil.ly/WkVJ4*) is a branch of the French Press Alliance, which is dedicated to fact-checking claims around the world. They select claims that have gained focus and assign them to a network of global fact-checking editors. The steps taken to verify the claim are stated in the final article that summarizes their research.

Unlike PolitiFact and Snopes, FactCheck.org and AFP Fact Check do not have a one-word rating on whether the statement is false or true. The readers will get to the conclusion by reading their summary. Often when there is no summary, the articles will summarize their conclusions in the first paragraph and then go on to elaborate on it (Figure 3-4).

Q: Did the government issue new dollar coins without the words "In God We Trust"?

A: Congress ordered the words to be stamped on the edges of the coins, but an unknown number of "Godless dollars" were produced by mistake.

Figure 3-4. The question-answer structure of the FactCheck.org page; retrieved from https://oreil.ly/qF0jZ

The logic used to scrape the websites is illustrated in the following code snippets:

```
def get_factcheck_first_paragraph(url):
    result = "abstain"
    try:
        parsed_html = get_parsed_html(url)
        div = parsed_html.body.find("div", attrs={"class":"entry-content"})
        # if the first paragraph starts with 'Q:'
        # and the second with 'A:' than it is a Q & A style;
        # take the second paragraph
        # otherwise take the first.
        parag = div.find_all("p")
        if (parag[0].text[0:3] == "Q: " and parag[1].text[0:3] == "A: "):
            return parag[1].text
        return parag[0].text
    except Exception as e:
        print(e)
    return result

def get_factcheck_afp_title(url):
    result = "abstain"
    try:
        parsed_html = get_parsed_html(url)
        h3 = parsed_html.body.find("h3")
        return h3.text
    except Exception as e:
        print(e)
    return result
```

One quick way to analyze whether the answer or the summary of the research is in agreement with the claim or not is to analyze the sentiment of this summary. Positive sentiment is an indicator of agreement, and negative sentiment is an indicator of disagreement, which we use to mark the statement as FAKE. We use the NLTK vader

Sentiment Intensity Analyzer (*https://oreil.ly/Xheod*) to get the negative and positive sentiment scores:

```
from nltk.sentiment.vader import SentimentIntensityAnalyzer
sid = SentimentIntensityAnalyzer()

sentiment = sid.polarity_scores(
"Immigration comments by Sen. Elizabeth"+
"Warren have been selectively edited in a misleading way"+
"and are circulating widely online.")
print(sentiment)
```

For example, analyzing one of the FactCheck.org answers to a claim present in the dataset detects a largely neutral sentence with a light negative sentiment:

```
{'neg': 0.144, 'neu': 0.856, 'pos': 0.0, 'compound': -0.4019}
```

The respective Snorkel labeling functions will act on the samples that have a FactCheck or AFP Fact Check sentiment score, and return REAL if the dominant sentiment is positive and FAKE if the dominant sentiment is negative; ABSTAIN if otherwise:

```
def factcheck_sentiment(row, columnName):
    label = str(row[columnName])
    score = 0
    if label:
        claims = label[1:-1].split(',')
        for claim in claims:
            sentiment = sid.polarity_scores(claim)
            if sentiment["neg"] > sentiment["pos"]:
                score -=1
            elif sentiment["pos"] > sentiment["neg"]:
                score +=1
        if score > 0:
            return REAL
        elif score < 0:
            return FAKE
        else:
            return ABSTAIN
    return ABSTAIN

@labeling_function()
def factcheckqa(row):
    return factcheck_sentiment(row, "www.factcheck.org")

@labeling_function()
def factcheckafpqa(row):
    return factcheck_sentiment(row, "factcheck.afp.com")
```

Crowdsourcing

The results from the other sources like "www.glennbeck.com," "www.washington-post.com/news/fact-checker," and "www.realclearpolitics.com" did not have this property of summarizing the claim in a consistently placed paragraph of the text, so to be able to convert the research article to a FAKE or REAL label, one has to…read the entire article. To scale reading and labeling the statements according to those few hundred articles, we resorted to crowdsourcing. The crowdsourcing results were appended to the dataset (this effort cost the authors of the book part of their end-of-year holiday season):

```
def crowdsourced(row, site):
    label = str(row[site])
    if label != "nan":
        if "real" in label:
            return REAL
        else:
            return FAKE
    else:
        return ABSTAIN

@labeling_function()
def label_gb(row):
    return crowdsourced(row, "www.glennbeck.com")

@labeling_function()
def label_wp(row):
    return crowdsourced(row, "www.washingtonpost.com/news/fact-checker")

@labeling_function()
def label_rp(row):
    return crowdsourced(row,"www.realclearpolitics.com")
```

Is the Speaker a "Liar"?

Another observation of Shu, Mahudeswaran, Wang, Lee, and Liu in their fake news research[5] was that the actual source of the statement was a good indicator of the truthfulness of a statement. Speakers that publish a high rate of statements deemed as false are more prone to doing so in the future than speakers having a higher rate of statements classified as correct. To learn the patterns of publishing fake/real statements for speakers, we turned to a similar labeled dataset: the "fake news detection(LIAR)." This dataset is part of FNID as well and is created at the same time as our "fake news detection(FakeNewsNet)." It follows the structure of LIAR dataset (*https://oreil.ly/MKeiO*), as shown in Table 3-2:

---

5 Shu et al., "FakeNewsNet: A Data Repository with News Content, Social Context and Spatialtemporal Information for Studying Fake News on Social Media."

```
liar = pd.read_csv(r"fake news detection(LIAR)\liar_train.csv")
liar.head(3)
```

Table 3-2. Preview of the "fake news detection(LIAR)" dataset

id	date	speaker	statement	sources	paragraph_based_content	label-liar
18178	2020-03-18	Instagram posts	"COVID-19 started because we eat animals."	['https://www.cdc.gov/coronavirus/2019-ncov/ca	['Vegan Instagram users are pinning the 2019 c.	barely-true
3350	2011-03-04	Glenn Beck	Says Michelle Obama has 43 people on her staff	['http://www.glennbeck.com/2011/02/25/while-wo...	['Glenn Beck rekindled a falsehood about the s...	pants-fire
14343	2017-07-21	Mike Pence	Says President Donald Trump "has signed more l...	['https://nrf.com/events/retail-advocates-summ...	['Vice President Mike Pence says that when it ...	half-true

Since this dataset is collected by crawling PolitiFact, the labels used for the claims are the Truth-O-Meter values mentioned previously:

```
# check the unique labels
labels = liar["label-liar"].unique()
labels
```

And the unique labels are:

```
array(['barely-true', 'pants-fire', 'half-true',
'mostly-true', 'true', 'false'], dtype=object)
```

We leveraged only the claims that were labeled as "true," "mostly-true," "false," and "pants-fire." We then calculated the percentage of times a speaker had statements rated in the two camps. The counts_true and counts_false contain those numbers, respectively, and the false_percent and true_percent contain those same values as percentages:

```
counts = {}
# true speakers
counts_true = collections.Counter(liar[(liar["label-liar"]=="mostly-true")
|(liar["label-liar"]=="true")]["speaker"])
counts_true = dict(counts_true.most_common())
# false speakers
counts_false = collections.Counter(liar[(liar["label-liar"]=="false" )
| (liar["label-liar"]=="pants-fire")]["speaker"])
counts_false = dict(counts_false.most_common())

false_percent = {}
for k, v in counts_false.items():
    total = v
```

```
        if k in counts_true:
            total += counts_true[k]
        false_percent[k] = v/total

    true_percent = {}
    for k, v in counts_true.items():
        total = v
        if k in counts_false:
            total += counts_false[k]
        true_percent[k] = v/total
```

The labeling function consists of comparing the percentages to 60%, and if the speaker has a higher than 60% history of speaking falsehood, this labeling_function votes for the article to be FAKE. Vice-versa if the percentage of true claims is higher than 60%:

```
@labeling_function()
def speaker(row):
    speaker = row["speaker"]
    if(speaker in true_percent and true_percent[speaker] > 0.6):
        return REAL
    if(speaker in false_percent and false_percent[speaker] > 0.6):
        return FAKE
    return ABSTAIN
```

Twitter Profile and Botometer Score

Some of the URLs in the source are from tweets about the news. One of the conclusions of Shu, Mahudeswaran, Wang, Lee, and Liu in their fake news research[6] indicated that the social media reaction around a statement is pretty telling about the veracity of the statement. Bots tend to amplify fake statements, and true people are more likely to amplify truthful statements. The Botomoter API (*https://botome ter.osome.iu.edu*) is a project of the Observatory on Social Media (*https:// osome.iu.edu*), from Indiana University, aiming at scoring the bot-ness of a fact account (is the account a bot or a human being?). One example of the information this report provides for a particular Twitter user can be seen in Figure 3-5.

Extracting the Botometer score for the Twitter URLs can serve as an additional labeling function for data points that have a tweet attached to them.

---

6 Shu et al., "FakeNewsNet: A Data Repository with News Content, Social Context and Spatialtemporal Information for Studying Fake News on Social Media."

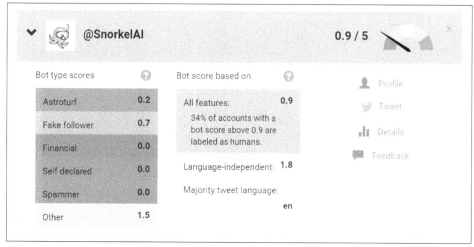

Figure 3-5. Preview of the "fake news detection(LIAR)" dataset

Generating Agreements Between Weak Classifiers

The next step toward labeling the data is aggregating all the votes from the labeling functions to create a weak label in a statistically meaningful way.

The first step would be to split the DataFrame into a train and validation fraction. We chose to do so in the 80%/20% ratio. The lfs array is a list of all the "labeling functions." The PandasLFApplier.apply will "apply" the labeling functions to the dataset to get their REAL, FAKE, or ABSTAIN vote:

```
data = data.sample(frac = 1, random_state = 1)
df_train = data[:12170]
df_valid = data[12170:]

lfs = [
        label_rp,
        label_wp,
        label_gb,
        label_snopes,
        label_politifact,
        factcheckqa,
        factcheckafpqa,
        speaker
    ]

applier = PandasLFApplier(lfs=lfs)
L_train = applier.apply(df=df_train)
LFAnalysis(L=L_train, lfs=lfs).lf_summary()
```

The LFAnalysis will analyze the output of the labeling functions in a matrix form (Table 3-3), including output Coverage, the fraction of data that the particular labeling function has labeled; `Overlaps`, the fraction of data on which this labeling function has overlapped with another labeling function; and `Conflict`, the fraction of data on which this labeling function has emitted a decision that was different from the decision of another labeling function.

Table 3-3. The df_val DataFrame

	Polarity	Coverage	Overlaps	Conflicts
label_rp	[0, 1]	0.0078	0.0069	0.0025
label_wp	[0, 1]	0.0102	0.0096	0.0035
label_gb	[0, 1]	0.0015	0.0014	0.0004
label_snopes	[0, 1]	0.0273	0.0265	0.0043
label_politifact	[0, 1]	0.2903	0.2164	0.0837
factcheckqa	[0, 1]	0.0202	0.0195	0.0113
factcheckafpqa	[0, 1]	0.0012	0.0012	0.0007
speaker	[0, 1]	0.7184	0.2451	0.0884

From the statistics, we can see that the highest coverage comes from the "label politifact," the PolitiFact ratings, and the `speaker` from our "fake news detection(LIAR)" transfer learning. Because of the higher Coverage, they also have higher Overlaps and higher Conflicts. The lower value labels are the ones having high Conflicts or low Overlaps compared with Coverage. None of our labeling functions seem to fall into that category.

Let's next train the `LabelModel` to learn how to best combine the output of the "labeling functions," and then generate predictions to be used as labels for the training data. Since we have the true labels for this dataset, we can also measure the Empirical Accuracy or the accuracy of our labeling function with regard to the ground truth:

```
label_model = LabelModel()
label_model.fit(L_train=L_train, n_epochs=100, log_freq=100, seed=123)
preds_train_label = label_model.predict(L=L_train)
preds_valid_label = label_model.predict(L=L_valid)
L_valid = applier.apply(df_valid)
Y_valid = df_valid["label_numeric"].values
LFAnalysis(L_valid, lfs).lf_summary(Y_valid)
```

The output of `LFAnalysis` on the validation set is presented in Table 3-4.

Table 3-4. The df_val DataFrame:

	Correct	Incorrect	Emp. Acc.
label_rp	29	0	1
label_wp	26	0	1
label_gb	3	0	1

	Correct	Incorrect	Emp. Acc.
label_snopes	68	4	0.94
label_politifact	549	348	0.61
factcheckqa	38	31	0.55
factcheckafpqa	1	3	0.25
speaker	1666	505	0.77

We can judge that the most correct labeling function comes from crowdsourcing, followed by the Snopes ratings. The next most accurate source comes from the speaker labeling function. This matches the observation of Shu, Mahudeswaran, Wang, Lee, and Liu. PolitiFact is only 61% accurate.

As we just observed, when looking at the labels generated for some of the records, the PolitiFact entries had quite conflicting signals for some of the samples due to the nuances in the statements. factcheckafpqa is rated at only 25% accuracy, but that metric is not very trustworthy as the number of samples in the validation set is quite low at only 4.

Another way to gauge the quality of the labeling functions and LabelModel, besides the Correct, Incorrect, and Empirical Accuracy statistics generated in the validation set, is to use well-known machine learning classification metrics.

Snorkel supports metrics out of the box, and it uses the same familiar names as the sklearn.metrics package. To calculate some of those metrics in the validation set, we would run the following:

```
accuracy = label_model.score(L_valid, Y_valid, metrics=["accuracy"])
recall = label_model.score(L_valid, Y_valid, metrics=["recall"])
precision = label_model.score(L_valid, Y_valid, metrics=["precision"])

print("{}\n{}\n{}".format(accuracy, recall, precision))
```

The accuracy, precision, and recall metrics are all in the 70% range:

```
{'accuracy' : 0.7548}
{'recall'   : 0.7738}
{'precision': 0.7356}
```

The predictions for the training and the validation set joined together will form the dataset that we will then go on to use to build deep learning models for this task in Chapter 4:

```
Snorkel_predictions = np.concatenate((preds_train_label,preds_valid_label))
data["Snorkel_labels"] = Snorkel_predictions
data.to_csv("data_nlp.csv")
```

Labeling an Images Dataset: Determining Indoor Versus Outdoor Images

In this section, we will illustrate how to go about putting together an images dataset from pictures of outdoor and indoor settings, and use Snorkel together with other computer vision tools and predictors to programmatically classify the images as either "indoor" or "outdoor."

The field of computer vision has made great progress after the conception of AlexNet and the advent of GPUs. One of the factors that allowed and fueled the innovation in the field was the existence of the ImageNet images dataset. The ImageNet dataset consists of 14 million hand-annotated images categorized in 22,000 different classes.[7] Having this large-scale labeled data was crucial to the creation of AlexNet and the continuous breakthroughs in the image classification task. AlexNet was followed by ZFNet, VGG, GoogLeNet, ResNet, SqueezeNet, DenseNet, Visual Transformers, and others.[8] In recent years, the classification error has been reduced from 30% to close to 3.5%. Human classification error is 5%.[9]

Building and labeling a dataset at the scale of ImageNet was a significant, multiparty effort initiated in 2008 by Fei-Fei Li at the Stanford Vision Lab. The two crucial parts of putting together this dataset were collecting the images and labeling the images. Labeling was made possible through crowdsourcing: distributing the images to human judges and using their judgments to determine the category the image belongs to.

With Snorkel, we can solve the problem of labeling images in a faster way. For this purpose, we, the authors, have created a dataset of indoor and outdoor images. You can download the dataset from the book's GitHub repo (*https://oreil.ly/SAajM*). Although the problem we are tackling seems simple, the methodology used should scale to the multiclass problem or problems beyond image classification.

Our dataset contains 2,044 images. They are labeled (separated into two folders named "indoor" and "outdoor"), but again, similar to the previous case with the text dataset, we only use these labels to calculate the empirical accuracy of our learned model on the validation set. The dataset was put together selecting the images with the help of Bing Search, and it is noisy. Not all the outdoor images selected as such by

---

7 Jia Deng et al. "ImageNet: A large-scale hierarchical image database" *2009 IEEE Conference on Computer Vision and Pattern Recognition* (2009): 248-255, *https://ieeexplore.ieee.org/document/5206848*.

8 Urmil Shah and Aishwarya Harpale, "A Review of Deep Learning Models for Computer Vision," *2018 IEEE Punecon* (2018): 1–6, *https://ieeexplore.ieee.org/document/8745417*.

9 Jie Hu et al., "Squeeze-and-Excitation Networks" (Preprint, submitted May 16, 2019), *https://arxiv.org/pdf/1709.01507v4*.

Bing Search are images a human would label as outdoor, and the same goes for the ones in the "indoor" category. For example, see the following images.

Figure 3-6 is collected in the search for outdoor images.

Figure 3-6. A noisy outdoor image (source: https://oreil.ly/ROusd)

This "outdoor" image probably came back in the search results because it seems associated with camping, an outdoor activity.

Figure 3-7 is probably taken from a cricket game played in a closed arena. The green of the field and the good illumination of the scene makes it difficult even for humans to distinguish whether it is truly indoor or outdoor.

Figure 3-7. A noisy indoor image (source: https://oreil.ly/9Rpvj)

But what makes us decide that an image is taken indoors or outdoors? Some of the dominant features of an outdoor image, taken in nature, are:

- The presence of the sky: blue for most days, potentially with clouds and the sun shining; it can also be dark blue or black at night with the stars and the moon present
- The green grass or a lot of vegetation
- Bodies of water like seas, rivers, lakes

For images taken outdoor in inhabited areas, like villages or cities, typical features would be:

- The presence of buildings
- Streets, vehicles

The indoor labels are a bit trickier because many different indoor settings don't share the same visual characteristics; for example, objects found in a school are very different from the objects found in a gym.

To illustrate this difference, Figure 3-8 shows the image of the inside view of a plane, and Figure 3-9 shows a traditional Japanese house. See how difficult it is to find visual commonalities between the two?

Figure 3-8. The inside of a Lufthansa plane (source: https://oreil.ly/98agm)

Figure 3-9. A traditional Japanese house (source: https://oreil.ly/iiqvh)

Nevertheless, we can attempt to train a few classifiers to recognize very common objects:

- Windows
- Floors
- Picture frames
- Basic furniture, like chairs and sofas

So a natural way to create weak classifiers to then use as labeling functions would be to create a series of binary classifiers that can recognize whether one of the elements mentioned in the preceding list is present in the picture or not. Concretely, we will train a binary classifier to recognize whether an image contains the sky or green grass or whether it contains furniture, windows, or picture frames. We will then use the Snorkel labeling framework to aggregate the signals from those classifiers. Specifically, we will treat these classifiers as labeling functions and learn a `LabelModel` (*https://oreil.ly/Wcxz2*) that can be used to estimate the true label for each data point that is covered by at least one labeling function.

To be able to train those classifiers to use as labeling functions, we first need data, and one way to get batches of images is through the search engine APIs, like the Bing Search Service (*https://oreil.ly/7yUcO*).

Creating a Dataset of Images from Bing

The Azure Cognitive Services Bing Search API enables searching the web for a particular type of media and a particular topic, similar to searching in the *www.bing.com* interface. This API enables quick and free data collection if you need to train auxiliary models for your weak supervision problems like we are doing for this indoor/outdoor classification problem.

For the collection of our images, we chose to use the *www.bing.com* interface, since that has the additional functionality to filter and display content based on the license. The images we selected have licenses that allow us to use them free for commercial purposes.

We saved the search results pages, which automatically saved the images in the folder, and programmatically copied them from there to another folder, repeating the process a few times for different outdoor and indoor themes, and then we merged all those images together.

Defining and Training Weak Classifiers in TensorFlow

Now that we have the images to train the classifiers, we can define a convolutional neural network (CNN) in one of the popular deep learning frameworks: TensorFlow (*https://www.tensorflow.org*) or PyTorch (*https://pytorch.org*). Both frameworks have well-documented APIs and a rich set of tutorials. For our classifiers, we are going to define and train the network using TensorFlow. The training and predicting code is largely based on the Image Classification TensorFlow tutorial (*https://oreil.ly/aOEzv*).

See Chapter 5 for details on how CNNs work. *Hands-On Convolutional Neural Networks with TensorFlow* (Packt, 2018) (*https://oreil.ly/1OiLJ*) is a book entirely dedicated to practical deep learning and convolutional neural networks.

Let's first install TensorFlow. In the Anaconda command prompt, you can type:

```
pip install tensorflow
```

Start the Jupyter service and create a new Python 3 Jupyter notebook. Import the packages:

```
import tensorflow as tf
from tensorflow import keras
from tensorflow.keras import layers
from tensorflow.keras.models import Sequential
import pathlib
```

The structure of the images folder, for one of the binary classifiers—the floor_binary folder—looks like this:

```
floor_binary /
..../floor
......../4.jpg
......../19.jpg
......../ ....
..../other
......../275.jpg
......../294.jpg
......../ ....
```

Load the list of image paths. This will be done for each folder containing the images for the training of the binary classifiers:

```
data_dir = pathlib.Path(r"<PATH TO ONE OF THE IMAGES FOLDER>")
image_list= list(data_dir.glob("*/*.jpg"))
```

Define the training function. `tf.keras` offers convenient APIs to load the data and resize them so they are all the same size: a requirement for the CNN input. The default image height and width is 256. The loading APIs also let you define the portion of the data to use for the training set and for the validation set. The default batch size for `tf.keras` is 32.

The class names are extracted from the names of the subfolders where the images live, and the data is cached to be in memory for the various epoch training. The CNN contains three convolutional layers, two max pooling layers, and the last softmax layer, which will yield the probabilities for each class:

```
'''
Define and train a convolutional neural network with 3
convolutional layers, 3 max-pooling layers
'''
def train_model(data_dir, epochs, seed):
    train_ds = tf.keras.preprocessing.image_dataset_from_directory(
        data_dir,
        validation_split= 0.2,
        subset= "training",
        seed= seed)
    val_ds = tf.keras.preprocessing.image_dataset_from_directory(
        data_dir,
        validation_split=0.2,
        subset= "validation",
        seed= seed)

    class_names = train_ds.class_names
    num_classes = len(class_names)
    print("Class names: {}".format(class_names))

    # cache the data, to have it readily available,
    # and to avoid reloading between epochs
    train_ds = train_ds.cache().shuffle(200).prefetch(buffer_size=200)

    multiclass_model = Sequential([
```

```python
    # rescale the vector of numbers representing color
    # from [0, 255] to [0, 1]
    layers.experimental.preprocessing.Rescaling(1./255),
    # define the convolutional layer, padding
    # and type of activation function
    layers.Conv2D(16, 3, padding="same", activation="relu"),
    layers.MaxPooling2D(),
    layers.Conv2D(32, 3, padding="same", activation="relu"),
    layers.MaxPooling2D(),
    layers.Conv2D(64, 3, padding="same", activation="relu"),
    layers.MaxPooling2D(),
    layers.Flatten(),
    layers.Dense(128, activation="relu"),
    layers.Dense(num_classes)
])

# compile the model, select the type of optimizer and
# the target metric
multiclass_model.compile(optimizer="adam",
    loss=tf.keras.losses.SparseCategoricalCrossentropy(from_logits=True),
    metrics=["accuracy"])

# fit the model
history = multiclass_model.fit(
    train_ds,
    validation_data=val_ds,
    epochs=epochs)

return multiclass_model
```

Let's now define the prediction function, which should take the path of a new image, the model, and the class names, and predict which class a given image belongs to. The target size is defined to be 256 for width and height because that is the default the Keras loading API resizes the images to:

```python
def predict(path, model, class_names, silent=True):
    # load the images
    img = tf.keras.preprocessing.image.load_img(path,
    target_size=(256, 256))
    img_array = tf.keras.preprocessing.image.img_to_array(img)
    img_array = tf.expand_dims(img_array, 0)

    predictions = model.predict(img_array)
    # get the predicted probabilities
    score = tf.nn.softmax(predictions[0])
    # get the class name corresponding to the element with the
    # highest probability, and convert it to percentage
    img_class = class_names[np.argmax(score)]
    prob = 100 * np.max(score)
    if not silent:
        print("This image most likely belongs to {} with a
        {:02f} percent confidence.".format(img_class, prob))
```

```
#return all probabilities, in case we want to evaluate
# if there is a close second
return score.numpy()
```

Training the Various Classifiers

We will now need to call the training function for each binary classifier folder of images so we can train each model. The resulting models will be stored in a dictionary to have them handy when creating the labeling functions.

The classes *array*
    Contains the names of each folder we will use to train a `binary_classifier`.

The test *array*
    Contains the names of the other images we will use to quickly validate our classifiers. The images can be found at *ch03_creating_datasets/cv/data/test* in the GitHub repository (*https://bit.ly/WeakSupervisionBook*).

The data_path
    The path where the images we will use to train the binary classifiers are stored. It corresponds to the *ch03_creating_datasets/cv/data/images* GitHub folder.

The test_path
    Corresponds to the *ch03_creating_datasets/cv/data/test* GitHub folder.

class_names
    A dictionary containing the correspondence class name: an array of labels. The array of labels is passed as an argument to the prediction function, and the positions of the labels: need to correspond to the class names used by the training function. As we previously mentioned, the training functions read the class names (the labels) from the folders in the file system, and therefore they are ordered alphabetically.

models
    A dictionary that holds the correspondence class name binary model:

```
classes = ["floor", "frame", "furniture","grass",
           "sea", "sky", "street", "window"]
test = ["guitar", "salad", "book", "cartoon"]
data_path = r"<DATA_PATH>"
test_path = r"<TEST_PATH>"

class_names = {
    "floor": ["floor", "other"],
    "frame": ["frame", "other"],
    "furniture": ["furniture", "other"],
    "grass": ["grass", "other"],
    "sea": ["other", "sea"],
    "sky": ["other", "sky"],
```

```
    "street": [ "other", "street"],
    "window": [ "other", "window"]
}

models = { }
```

We then train each binary classifier, as follows:

```
for c in classes:
    model = train_model(os.path.join(data_path, str(c)+"_binary"), 10, 456)
    models[c] = model
    print("Predictions are for model {0}."+
    "The first one is the positive class,"+
    "and the second one the negative class".format(c))
    # Trying out prediction for the positive class
    predict(os.path.join(test_path, str(c)+".jpg"), model, class_names[c])
    # trying out prediction for another image, selected at random from
    # the pool of the images in the test folder
    predict(os.path.join(test_path, test[np.random.randint(0, 3)]+".jpg"),
    model, class_names[c])
```

The output for one such classifier, the one learning to predict whether the image contains a floor, is as follows:

```
Found 291 files belonging to 2 classes.
Using 233 files for training.
Found 291 files belonging to 2 classes.
Using 58 files for validation.
Class names: ["floor", "other"]
Epoch 1/10
8/8 [==============================] - 3s 368ms/step - loss: 1.2747
- accuracy: 0.4979 - val_loss: 0.6863 - val_accuracy: 0.5000
Epoch 2/10
8/8 [==============================] - 3s 342ms/step - loss: 0.6769
- accuracy: 0.5536 - val_loss: 0.6138 - val_accuracy: 0.6897
Epoch 3/10
8/8 [==============================] - 3s 334ms/step - loss: 0.6151
- accuracy: 0.6867 - val_loss: 0.6621 - val_accuracy: 0.5172
Epoch 4/10
8/8 [==============================] - 3s 360ms/step - loss: 0.5895
- accuracy: 0.6824 - val_loss: 0.6642 - val_accuracy: 0.5345
Epoch 5/10
8/8 [==============================] - 3s 318ms/step - loss: 0.5630
- accuracy: 0.6953 - val_loss: 0.4029 - val_accuracy: 0.8276
Epoch 6/10
8/8 [==============================] - 3s 342ms/step - loss: 0.3475
- accuracy: 0.8884 - val_loss: 0.2502 - val_accuracy: 0.8793
Epoch 7/10
8/8 [==============================] - 3s 380ms/step - loss: 0.3351
- accuracy: 0.8712 - val_loss: 0.2947 - val_accuracy: 0.8966
Epoch 8/10
8/8 [==============================] - 3s 323ms/step - loss: 0.2387
- accuracy: 0.9056 - val_loss: 0.3761 - val_accuracy: 0.8103
```

```
Epoch 9/10
8/8 [==============================] - 3s 395ms/step - loss: 0.1806
- accuracy: 0.9399 - val_loss: 0.2485 - val_accuracy: 0.8966
Epoch 10/10
8/8 [==============================] - 3s 369ms/step - loss: 0.1173
- accuracy: 0.9700 - val_loss: 0.2386 - val_accuracy: 0.8621

Predictions are for model floor.
The first one is the positive class, and the second one the negative class
Found 236 files belonging to 2 classes.
Using 189 files for training.
Found 236 files belonging to 2 classes.
Using 47 files for validation.
Class names: ["frame", "other"]
```

Looking at the accuracy for each classifier, it seems like they are doing reasonably well, although the pool of images they used for training was pretty small. To have better classifiers, we could increase the number of images we supply to training.

 A nice exercise for the reader would be to come up with other classes of objects that define indoor and outdoor, collect the respective images, and train additional classifiers.

Now that we have a pool of binary classifiers, we are going to proceed with creating the labeling functions and attempting to label our images. To increase our chances for success, we will attempt to gather more information about the images by using a service that describes the subject of the image.

Weak Classifiers out of Image Tags

Services that take as input an image and return a description of what they "see" in the image typically use pretrained image recognition models. Those models detect various regions or objects in the image and return the descriptions for these objects or regions. The Azure Computer Vision Service (*https://oreil.ly/I7iHq*) is one such service offering image understanding. The model behind it is based on an ontology of 10,000 concepts and objects. You can submit a picture to it, either as the base64 encoded image, or a URL to a publicly available image. Then it will return the list of objects it has recognized in the picture, a name for those objects, and the bounding boxes of where the object is located in the image, as well as the confidence on the detection.

One of our labeling functions will inspect this group of tags and look for the *outdoor* and *indoor* tags.

Deploying the Computer Vision Service

If you don't have an Azure subscription, you can still try the Computer Vision Service for free (*https://oreil.ly/pOK8U*), as you can see in Figure 3-10.

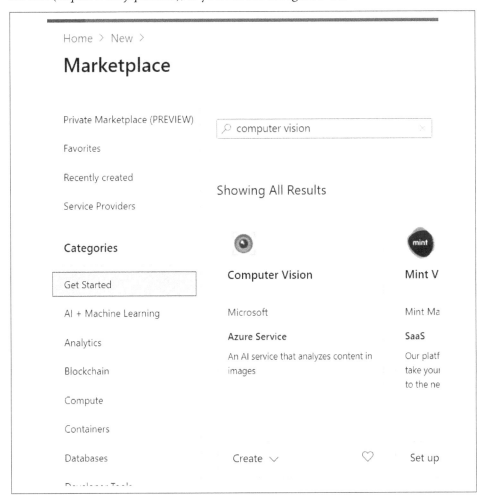

Figure 3-10. The Computer Vision Azure service

The service deployment takes a couple of minutes. After the service is up and running, take note of the endpoint and the key, as you will need them to initialize the Python client to connect to the service and post the images. They are found in the "Keys and Endpoint" tab, as you can see in Figure 3-11.

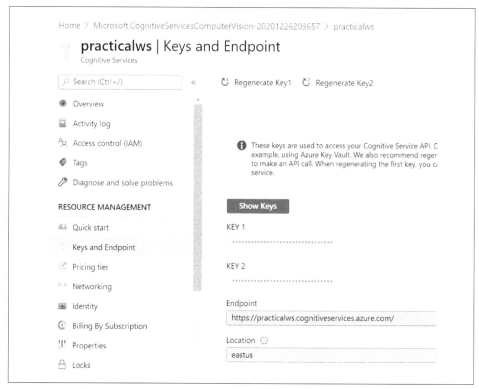

Figure 3-11. The Keys and Endpoint of the Computer Vision Azure service

Interacting with the Computer Vision Service

The `azure-cognitiveservices-vision-computervision` is the Python package that serves as a client to the Azure Computer Vision Service:

```
pip install --upgrade azure-cognitiveservices-vision-computervision
```

The packages to import in order to call the Computer Vision service are:

```
from azure.cognitiveservices.vision.computervision import
ComputerVisionClient
from azure.cognitiveservices.vision.computervision.models import
OperationStatusCodes
from azure.cognitiveservices.vision.computervision.models import
VisualFeatureTypes
from msrest.authentication import CognitiveServicesCredentials

from array import array
import os
import sys
import time
```

In the deployed service, you can find the key and the endpoint of your service. Copy those values, and place them in the subscription_key and endpoint variables, respectively, to create the ComputerVisionClient:

```
subscription_key = "<KEY>"
endpoint = "<ENDPOINT>"
computervision_client = ComputerVisionClient(endpoint,
CognitiveServicesCredentials(subscription_key))
```

 If you are working on an enterprise project, where secrets cannot live in the notebook or in your local machine, you can use the Azure Jupyter Notebook that comes with an Azure Machine Learning workspace and store the secrets in the Key Vault. See "Use authentication credential secrets in Azure Machine Learning training runs" (*https://oreil.ly/547hS*) for enterprise best practices.

The computervision_client object submits the image to Cognitive Service API, which in turn will generate a set of tags describing the image. The describe_image function then returns a list of the names of the tags generated:

```
# Call the Cognitive Services API
def describe_image(x):
    tags = computervision_client.tag_image(x).tags
    return [tag.name for tag in tags]
```

Next, we need to put together a DataFrame, containing the paths of the images. We are doing so now so that we have a place to keep the association of the labels we will receive with the actual path of the images.

Let's iterate over all the pictures in the images folder, capture their path, and make that the first column of the DataFrame:

```
data_dir = pathlib.Path(r"<PATH OF THE FINAL FOLDER>")
image_list= list(data_dir.glob("*/*.jpg"))
# let's shuffle the images
random.shuffle(image_list)
df = pd.DataFrame(image_list, columns = ["Path"])
df.head(3)
```

After executing the preceding snippet, we will have a DataFrame that looks like this:

```
Path

0       C:\images\outdoor\378.jpg
1       C:\images\indoor\763.jpg
2       C:\images\outdoor\85.jpg
```

To make use of the Azure ComputerVisionClient efficiently, we can have the images somewhere on the web or in a public location so we can supply the URL to the ComputerVisionClient (*https://oreil.ly/7QcOg*) tag_image (*https://oreil.ly/ynMqb*) API.

If you don't want to upload the images somewhere because you might have constraints on doing so, you can also use the `tag_image_in_stream` (*https://oreil.ly/vV4uw*) API, which will upload the image to tag, but the process will be slower.

If you upload the images folder as it is, preserving the directory structure as it is, you can have a variable for the base images URL and use the path of the images to compose the full URL to the image:

```
images/
..../indoor
......../763.jpg
......../....
..../outdoor
......../85.jpg
```

At the time of this writing, the Computer Vision API currently has a free SKU if you query for less than 20 pictures per minute and less than 5,000 pictures per month. To use this S0 SKU, and since time is not critical for this project, the following snippet of code is building a one-minute delay after getting a response:

```
base_storage_url = "<URL of the images folder>"
tags = [None] * df.size

# inquire for 20 images a minute, then pause,
# because that is the protocol with the free version of the
# Computer Vision API

for i, row in df.iterrows():
        tags[i] = describe_image(base_storage_url+df["rel_url"][i])
        print("counter: {0}. Tags {1}".format(i, tags[i]))
        if(i % 20 == 0):
            time.sleep(60)
```

Preparing the DataFrame

Next, let's attach the array of tags to the DataFrame. Given that we do know the labels for the images (because the images are split between the "indoor" and "outdoor" folders), we will extract the labels in a third column, which we will only use on the validation subset, to calculate the empirical accuracy:

```
# attach the tags array
df["tags"] = tags

# extract the label
df["label"] = df.apply(lambda x: INDOOR if "indoor" in str(x["Path"])
else OUTDOOR) , axis=1)

df.head(3)
```

The DataFrame would look similar to what's shown in Table 3-5.

Table 3-5. The DataFrame containing the output of the Computer Vision API tags

Path	Tags
C:\images\outdoor\378.jpg,1"	[outdoor, sky, ground, mountain…"
C:\images\indoor\763.jpg,-1,"	[indoor, sink, cabinetry, home …"
C:\images\outdoor\261.jpg,1,"	[tree, outdoor, grass, bicycle …"

Learning a LabelModel

Now that we have all the Python routines to use as heuristics, let's start by defining the labeling functions. Similar to what we did in Chapter 2, and the first part of this chapter, let's import the relevant Snorkel packages first:

```
from snorkel.labeling import labeling_function
from snorkel.labeling import PandasLFApplier
from snorkel.labeling import LFAnalysis
from snorkel.labeling.model import LabelModel
```

Next, let's define the numbers representing the INDOOR, OUTDOOR, and ABSTAIN labels:

```
ABSTAIN = -1
INDOOR = 0
OUTDOOR = 1

indoor = ["floor", "frame", "furniture","window"]
outdoor = ["grass", "sea", "sky", "street"]

def has_element(image_path, class_name):
    if class_name not in classes:
        raise Exception("Unsupported class")

    model = models[class_name]
    score = predict(image_path, model, class_names[class_name])
    predicted_class = class_names[class_name][np.argmax(score)]
    confidence = np.max(score)
    if predicted_class == class_name and confidence > 0.5:
        ret = INDOOR if class_name in indoor else OUTDOOR
        return ret
    else:
        return ABSTAIN
```

It is handy to define the indoor and outdoor strings used to key the models and the class names in respective arrays. The has_element function takes as parameters the path of the image and the name of a category, and then predicts the likelihood that the image belongs to that category. If the model predicts that the image belongs to that category with a probability higher than 50%, then has_element will return the name of the group to which the class belongs, respectively INDOOR or OUTDOOR:

```
@labeling_function()
def has_grass(x):
    return has_element(x["Path"], "grass")

@labeling_function()
def has_floor(x):
    return has_element(x["Path"], "floor")

@labeling_function()
def has_furniture(x):
    return has_element(x["Path"], "furniture")

@labeling_function()
def has_frame(x):
    return has_element(x["Path"], "frame")

@labeling_function()
def has_window(x):
    return has_element(x["Path"], "window")

@labeling_function()
def has_sea(x):
    return has_element(x["Path"], "sea")

@labeling_function()
def has_sky(x):
    return has_element(x["Path"], "sky")

@labeling_function()
def has_street(x):
    return has_element(x["Path"], "street")
```

The labeling functions would then be predicting for each image and for each category. Snorkel should then be able to learn that the images that have "sea" and "sky" on them are outdoor images, and the ones with "frames" and "furniture" are indoor images:

```
@labeling_function()
def is_outdoor(x):
    if "outdoor" in x["tags"]:
        return OUTDOOR

    if "indoor" in x["tags"]:
        return INDOOR

    return ABSTAIN
```

The labeling function making use of tags is different. If we look at the output of the Computer Vision API in Table 3-5, among the tags we encounter often are the actual "outdoor" and "indoor" tags. One heuristic would be to look for those particular keywords about the tags describing the image. Other effective labeling functions would look for keywords related to outdoors, like "mountains," "trees," "cars," or similarly for keywords typically describing indoors, like "sofa," "bed," "TV," and vote for those images to be labeled as indoor. Adding classifiers related to those tags would be a nice exercise for the reader to try out.

Next, let's split the dataset 80%/20% in a training (80%) and validation (20%) set. lfs defines the list of labeling functions to use in the voting process. We then create a PandasLFApplier(lfs), which we'll next apply to each portion of the dataset. The heuristic will "cast their vote," which we can then examine with the help of LfAnalysis:

```
df_train = df[0:1635]
df_valid = df[1636:2043]

lfs = [ has_grass,
        has_floor,
        has_furniture,
        has_frame,
        has_window,
        has_sea,
        has_sky,
        has_street,
        is_outdoor
      ]

applier = PandasLFApplier(lfs)
L_train = applier.apply(df_train)
L_valid = applier.apply(df_valid)

LFAnalysis(L_valid, lfs).lf_summary()
```

LFAnalysis.lf_summary() prints a summary of how each labeling heuristic performed, as shown in Table 3-6.

Table 3-6. The LFAnalysis summary DataFrame

	Polarity	Coverage	Overlaps	Conflicts
has_grass	[1]	0.5553	0.5528	0.3047
has_floor	[0]	0.5921	0.5921	0.3784
has_furniture	[0]	0.6511	0.6511	0.4226
has_frame	[0]	0.1794	0.1794	0.1056
has_window	[0]	0.2973	0.2973	0.1744
has_sea	[1]	0.4717	0.4717	0.2457
has_sky	[1]	0.2948	0.2948	0.1081
has_street	[1]	0.3120	0.3096	0.1056
is_outdoor	[0, 1]	0.8182	0.8157	0.3882

If we look at the Polarity column, the is_outdoor is the only labeling function that has voted for images to be both outdoors and indoors, which matches the logic in the function.

Next, let's look at the Coverage column. We know that our dataset is balanced because we constructed the dataset. The coverage for the has_grass labeling function is about 55%. That is not surprising, as many of the indoor pictures might have plants in the pictures. It also has 30% conflicts, indicating that it might indeed be voting "outdoors" for pictures that are getting an "indoor" vote from the other functions, likely on indoor images with plants.

has_furniture and has_floor are higher than expected at 65% and 59%, respectively. Those functions are probably mislabeling images. They also have 42% and 37% conflicts, another indication that they might not be the most useful functions.

has_frame and has_window have a coverage of 18% and 30%, respectively. The low coverage also explains the low amount of conflicts and overlaps: those two functions are abstaining a lot. Given the way those labeling functions are created, the overlap value should be high because they are generic enough and, for every record, at least another two to three functions should vote the same way. The functions with low coverage and the functions with high conflicts are probably the ones to rework or even decide to remove from the framework.

It is surprising to see that the has_sky function has only 31% coverage. All the outdoor images, in general, have some portion of the sky depicted.

Since we know the actual labels from those images from the way the dataset got assembled, we can go on and calculate the empirical accuracy and gain further visibility on the performance of the labeling strategies:

```
Y_valid = df_valid["label"].values
LFAnalysis(L_valid, lfs).lf_summary(Y_valid)
```

The result of running LFAnalysis on the validation set is illustrated in Table 3-7.

Table 3-7. The LFAnalysis summary DataFrame

	Correct	Incorrect	Emp. Acc.
has_grass	151	0	0.668142
has_floor	0	76	0.000000
has_furniture	0	88	0.000000
has_frame	0	12	0.000000
has_window	0	29	0.000000
has_sea	130	0	0.677083
has_sky	102	0	0.850000

	Correct	Incorrect	Emp. Acc.
has_street	95	0	0.748031
is_outdoor	171	6	0.513514

As we suspected from the Overlaps/Conflicts ratio and preceding analysis, has_furni
ture and has_floor are highly inaccurate. Similarly, the rate of coverage and conflicts for has_frame and has_window is at 1.5:1 or at 2:1.

Although there are no hard rules about what ratios indicate a good or a bad result, the
accuracy for a unipolar labeling function (labeling function that only labels one class)
should always be better than chance.

This is actually not surprising, given the number of samples we used to train those
models and the level of variation that there is in images for those classes. There are
many types of windows: their shapes, dimensions, curtains. Learning to classify furniture is equally challenging and practically impossible to achieve with a handful of
samples.

Learning to recognize fields of grass, sky, and vast amounts of water is a more attaina-
ble goal. The outdoor labeling functions do perform well.

Calculating the accuracy of the LabelingModel gives 75.4%:

```
accuracy = label_model.score(L_valid, Y_valid, metrics=["accuracy"])
```

```
{'accuracy': 0.75377}
```

Given that our image classifiers used for the labeling functions were trained on small
sets of data, and the fact that we were only looking for the words *outdoor* or *indoor*
among the tags returned by the Computer Vision API, for the other two labeling
functions an accuracy of 75% is pretty good.

It would not be hard to improve upon it following the same principles and build sim-
pler image classifiers with more data or add more labeling functions that look for
more tags related to outdoor and indoor, among other tags returned from the Computer Vision API.

Summary

In this chapter, we used Snorkel to rapidly label two datasets: one text dataset containing a series of statements that we needed to label as Real or Fake, and one consist-
ing of images that we needed to label as Outdoor or Indoor.

There are many ways to program heuristics and many strategies to label part of the
data. Snorkel provides a framework for efficiently aggregating those weak sources of
opinions into one label. Snorkel also provides the tools necessary to evaluate how the

labeling functions are doing, such as through the Coverage, Overlaps, and Conflicts reports.

Finally, having a portion of your data labeled is helpful to further analyze the performance of the Snorkel `LabelModel` and enable the type of rapid iteration on constituent labeling functions that can lead to performance improvement in practice.

## CHAPTER 4

Using the Snorkel-Labeled Dataset for Text Classification

The key ingredient for supervised learning is a labeled dataset. Weakly supervised techniques provide machine learning practitioners with a powerful approach for getting the labeled datasets that are needed to train natural language processing (NLP) models.

In Chapter 3, you learned how to use Snorkel to label the data from the FakeNewsNet dataset. In this chapter, you will learn how to use the following Python libraries for performing text classification using the weakly labeled dataset, produced by Snorkel:

ktrain
> At the beginning of this chapter, we first introduce the *ktrain* library. *ktrain* is a Python library that provides a lightweight wrapper for transformer-based models and enables anyone (including someone new to NLP) a gentle introduction to NLP.

Hugging Face
> Once you are used to the different NLP concepts, we will learn how to unleash the powerful capabilities of the *Hugging Face* library.

By using both *ktrain* and pretrained models from the *Hugging Face* libraries, we hope to help you get started by providing a gentle introduction to performing text classification on the weakly labeled dataset before moving on to use the full capabilities of the *Hugging Face* library.

We included a section showing you how you can deal with a class-imbalanced dataset. While the FakeNewsNet dataset used in this book is not imbalanced, we take you through the exercise of handling the class imbalance to help you build up the skills, and prepare you to be ready when you actually have to deal with a class-imbalanced dataset in the future.

Getting Started with Natural Language Processing (NLP)

NLP enables one to automate the processing of text data in tasks like parsing sentences to extract their grammatical structure, extracting entities from documents, classifying documents into categories, document ranking for retrieving the most relevant documents, summarizing documents, answering questions, translating documents, and more. The field of NLP has been continuously evolving and has made significant progress in recent years.

 For a theoretical and practical introduction to NLP, the books *Foundations of Natural Language Processing* by Christopher D. Manning and Hinrich Schütze and *Natural Language Processing with Python* (*https://www.nltk.org/book*) by Steven Bird, Ewan Klein, and Edward Loper will be useful.

Sebastian Ruder and his colleagues' 2019 tutorial "Transfer Learning in Natural Language Processing"[1] will be a great resource to help you get started if you are looking to jumpstart your understanding of the exciting field of NLP. In the tutorial, Ruder and colleagues shared a comprehensive overview of how transfer learning for NLP works. Interested readers should view this tutorial (*https://bit.ly/2QkBRVm*).

The goal of this chapter is to show how you can leverage NLP libraries for performing text classification using a labeled dataset produced by Snorkel. This chapter is not meant to demonstrate how weak supervision enables application debugging or supports iterative error analsysis with the Snorkel model that is provided. Readers should refer to the Snorkel documentation and tutorials to learn more.

Let's get started by learning about how transformer-based approaches have enabled transfer learning for NLP and how we can use it for performing text classification using the Snorkel-labeled FakeNewsNet dataset.

---

1 Sebastian Ruder et al., "Transfer Learning in Natural Language Processing," Slide presentation, Conference of the North American Chapter of the Association for Computational Linguistics [NAACL-HLT], Minneapolis, MN, June 2, 2019, *https://oreil.ly/5hyM8*.

Transformers

Transformers have been the key catalyst for many innovative NLP applications. In a nutshell, a transformer enables one to perform sequence-to-sequence tasks by leveraging a novel self-attention technique.

Transformers use a novel architecture that does not require a recurrent neural network (RNN) or convolutional neural network (CNN). In the paper "Attention Is All You Need" (*https://oreil.ly/j1G6f*), the authors showed how transformers outperform both recurrent and convolutional neural network approaches.

One of the popular transformer-based models, which uses a left/right language modeling objective, was described in the paper "Improving Language Understanding by Generative Pre-Training" (*https://oreil.ly/PvMzR*). Over the last few years, Bidirectional Encoder Representations from Transformers (BERT) has inspired many other transformer-based models. The paper "BERT: Pre-training of Deep Bidirectional Transformers for Language Understanding" (*https://oreil.ly/mWbaB*) provides a good overview of how BERT works. BERT has inspired an entire family of transformer-based approaches for pretraining language representations. This ranges from the different sizes of pretrained BERT models (from tiny to extremely large), including RoBERTa, ALBERT, and more.

To understand how transformers and self-attention work, the following articles provide a good read:

"A Primer in BERTology: What We Know About How BERT Works"[2]
  This is an extensive survey of more than 100+ studies of the BERT model.

"Transformers from Scratch" by Peter Bloem[3]
  To understand why self-attention works, Peter Bloem provided a good, simplified discussion in this article.

"The Illustrated Transformer" by Jay Alammar[4]
  This is a good read on understanding how Transformers work.

---

2 Anna Rogers, Olga Kovaleva, and Anna Rumshisky, "A Primer in BERTology: What We Know About How BERT Works" (Preprint, submitted November 9, 2020), *https://arxiv.org/abs/2002.12327*.

3 Peter Bloem, "Transformers from Scratch," *Peter Bloem* (blog), video lecture, August 18, 2019, *http://peter bloem.nl/blog/transformers*.

4 Jay Alammar, "The Illustrated Transformer," *jalammar.github* (blog), June 27, 2018, *http://jalammar.github.io/ illustrated-transformer*.

"Google AI Blog: Transformer: A Novel Neural Network Architecture for Language Understanding"[5]

Blog from Google AI that provides a good overview of the Transformer.

Motivated by the need to reduce the size of a BERT model, Victor Sanh, Lysandre Debut, Julien Chaumond, and Thomas Wolf[6] proposed DistilBERT, a language model that is 40% smaller and yet retains 97% of BERT's language understanding capabilities. Consequently, this enables DistilBERT to perform at least 60% faster.

Many novel applications and evolutions of transformer-based approaches are continuously being made available. For example, OpenAI used transformers to create language models in the form of GPT (*https://oreil.ly/44Ya3*) via unsupervised pretraining. These language models are then fine-tuned for a specific downstream task.[7] More recent transformer innovation includes GPT3 and Switch Transformers.

In this chapter, you will learn how to use the following transformer-based models for text classification:

- "DistilBERT, a Distilled Version of BERT: Smaller, Faster, Cheaper and Lighter" (*https://oreil.ly/Y3d4b*)
- "RoBERTa: A Robustly Optimized BERT Pretraining Approach" (*https://oreil.ly/1yya6*)

We will fine-tune the pretrained DistilBert and RoBERTa models and use them for performing text classification on the FakeNewsNet dataset. To help everyone jump-start, we will start the text classification exercise by using *ktrain*. Once we are used to the steps for training transformer-based models (e.g., fine-tuning DistilBert using *ktrain*), we will learn how to tap the full capabilities of *Hugging Face*. *Hugging Face* is a popular Python NLP library, which provides a rich collection of pretrained models and more than 12,638 models (as of July 2021) on their model hub.

In this chapter, we will use *Hugging Face* for training the RoBERTa model (*https://oreil.ly/1yya6*) and fine-tune it for the text classification task. Let's get started!

---

5 Jakob Uszkoreit, "Transformer: A Novel Neural Network Architecture for Language Understanding," *Google AI Blog*, August 31, 2017, *https://ai.googleblog.com/2017/08/transformer-novel-neural-network.html*.

6 Victor Sanh et al., "DistilBERT, A Distilled Version of BERT: Smaller, Faster, Cheaper and Lighter" (Preprint, submitted March 1, 2020), *https://arxiv.org/abs/1910.01108*.

7 Alec Radford et al., "Improving Language Understanding by Generative Pre-Training" (Preprint, submitted 2018), OpenAI, University of British Columbia, accessed August 13, 2021, *https://www.cs.ubc.ca/~amuham01/LING530/papers/radford2018improving.pdf*.

Hard Versus Probabilistic Labels

In Chapter 3, we learned how we can use Snorkel to produce the labels for the dataset that will be used for training. As noted by the authors of the "Snorkel Intro Tutorial: Data Labeling" (*https://oreil.ly/maWIU*), the goal is to be able to leverage the labels from each of the Snorkel labeling functions and convert them into a single noise-aware probabilistic (or confidence-weighted) label.

In this chapter, we use the FakeNewsNet dataset and label that has been labeled by Snorkel in Chapter 3. This Snorkel label is referred to as a column, called `snorkel_labels` in the rest of this chapter.

Similar to the Snorkel Spam Tutorial, we will use `snorkel.labeling.MajorityLabel Voter`. The labels are produced by using the `predict()` method of `snorkel.label ing.MajorityLabelVoter`. From the documentation (*https://bit.ly/2Wlf02o*), the `predict()` method returns the predicted labels, which are returned as an ndarray of integer labels. In addition, the method supports different policies for breaking ties (e.g., abstain and random). By default, the abstain policy is used.

It is important to note that the Snorkel labeling functions (LFs) may be correlated. This might cause a majority-vote-based model to overrepresent some of the signals.

To address this, the `snorkel.labeling.model.label_model.LabelModel` can be used. The `predict()` method of `LabelModel` returns an ndarray of integer labels and an ndarray of probabilistic labels (if `return_probs` is set to True). These probabilistic labels can be used to train a classifier.

You can modify the code discussed in this chapter to use the probabilistic labels provided by `LabelModel` as well. *Hugging Face* implementation of transformers provide the `BCEWithLogitsLoss` function, which can be used with the probabilistic labels. (See the *Hugging Face* code for RoBERTa (*https://oreil.ly/cLA40*) to understand the different loss functions supported.)

For simplicity, this chapter uses the label outputs from `MajorityLabelVoter`.

Using ktrain for Performing Text Classification

To help everyone get started, we will use the Python library *ktrain* to illustrate how to train a transformer-based model. *ktrain* enables anyone to get started with using a transformer-based model quickly. *ktrain* enables us to leverage the pretrained Distil-BERT models (available in *Hugging Face*) to perform text classification.

Data Preparation

We load the *fakenews_snorkel_labels.csv* file and show the first few rows of the dataset:

```
import pandas as pd

# Read the FakeNewsNet dataset and show the first few rows
fakenews_df = pd.read_csv('../data/fakenews_snorkel_labels.csv')
fakenews_df[['id', 'statement','snorkel_labels']].head()
```

Let's first take a look at some of the columns in the FakeNewsNet dataset as shown in Table 4-1. For text classification, we will be using the columns `statement` and `snorkel_labels`. A value of 1 indicates it is real news, and 0 indicates it is fake news.

Table 4-1. Rows from the FakeNewsNet dataset

id	statement	...	snorkel_label
1248	During the Reagan era, while productivity incr...	...	1
4518	"It costs more money to put a person on death ...	...	1
15972	Says that Minnesota Democratic congressional c...	...	0
11165	"This is the most generous country in the worl...	...	1
14618	"Loopholes in current law prevent 'Unaccompani...	...	0

In the dataset, you will notice a –1 value in `snorkel_labels`. This is a value set by Snorkel when it is unsure of the label. We will remove rows that have `snorkel_values = -1` using the following code:

```
fakenews_df = fakenews_df[fakenews_df['snorkel_labels'] >= 0]
```

Next, let's take a look at the unique labels in the dataset:

```
# Get the unique labels
categories = fakenews_df.snorkel_labels.unique()
categories
```

The code produces the following output:

```
array([1, 0])
```

Let's understand the number of occurrences of real news (1) versus fake news (0). We use the following code to get the `value_counts` of fakenews_df[*label*]. This helps you understand how the real news versus fake news data is distributed and whether the dataset is imbalanced:

```
# count the number of rows with label 0 or 1
fakenews_df['snorkel_labels'].value_counts()
```

The code produces the following output:

```
1    6287
0    5859
Name: snorkel_labels, dtype: int64
```

Next, we will split the dataset into training and testing data. We used `train_test_split` from `sklearn.model_selection`. The dataset is split into 70% training data and 30% testing data. In addition, we initialize the random generator seed to be 98052. You can set the random generator seed to any value. Having a fixed value for the seed enables the results of your experiment to be reproducible in multiple runs:

```
# Prepare training and test data
from sklearn.model_selection import train_test_split

X = fakenews_df['statement']

# get the labels
labels = fakenews_df.snorkel_labels

# Split the data into train/test datasets
X_train, X_test, y_train, y_test = train_test_split(X,
                  labels,
                  test_size=0.30,
                  random_state=98052)
```

Let's count the number of labels in the training dataset:

```
# Count of label 0 and 1 in the training dataset
print("Rows in X_train %d : " % len(X_train))
type(X_train.values.tolist())

y_train.value_counts()
```

The code produces the following output:

```
Rows in X_train 8502 :
1    4395
0    4107
Name: snorkel_labels, dtype: int64
```

Dealing with an Imbalanced Dataset

While the data distribution for this current dataset does not indicate an imbalanced dataset, we included a section on how to deal with the imbalanced dataset, which we hope will be useful for you in future experiments where you have to deal with one.

In many real-world cases, the dataset is imbalanced. That is, there are more instances of one class (majority class) than the other class (minority class). In this section, we show how you can deal with class imbalance.

There are different approaches to dealing with the imbalanced dataset. One of the most commonly used techniques is resampling. In resampling, the data from the majority class are undersampled, and the data from the minority class are oversampled. In this way, you get a balanced dataset that has equal occurrences of both classes.

In this exercise, we will use `imblearn.under_sampling.RandomUnderSampler`. This approach will perform random undersampling of the majority class. Before using `imblearn.under_sampling.RandomUnderSampler`, we will need to prepare the data so it is in the input shape expected by `RandomUnderSampler`:

```
# Getting the dataset ready for using RandomUnderSampler
import numpy as np

X_train_np = X_train.to_numpy()
X_test_np =  X_test.to_numpy()

# Convert 1D to 2D (used as input to sampler)
X_train_np2D = np.reshape(X_train_np,(-1,1))
X_test_np2D = np.reshape(X_test_np,(-1,1))
```

Once the data is in the expected shape, we use `RandomUnderSampler` to perform undersampling of the training dataset:

```
from imblearn.under_sampling import RandomUnderSampler

# Perform random under-sampling
sampler = RandomUnderSampler(random_state = 98052)
X_train_rus, Y_train_rus = sampler.fit_resample(X_train_np2D, y_train)
X_test_rus, Y_test_rus = sampler.fit_resample(X_test_np2D, y_test)
```

The results are returned in the variables `X_train_rus` and `Y_train_rus`. Let's count the number of occurrences:

```
from collections import Counter

print('Resampled Training dataset  %s' % Counter(Y_train_rus))
print('Resampled Test dataset %s' % Counter(Y_test_rus))
```

In the results, you will see that the number of occurrences for both labels 0 and 1 in the training and test datasets are now balanced:

```
Resampled Training dataset  Counter({0: 4107, 1: 4107})
Resampled Test dataset Counter({0: 1752, 1: 1752})
```

Before we start training, we first flatten both training and testing datasets:

```
# Preparing the resampled datasets
# Flatten train and test dataset

X_train_rus = X_train_rus.flatten()
X_test_rus = X_test_rus.flatten()
```

Training the Model

In this section, we will be using *ktrain* to train a DistilBert model using the Fake-NewsNet dataset.

We will be using *ktrain* to train the text classification model. ktrain (*https://oreil.ly/9tPQu*) provides a lightweight *Tensorflow Keras* wrapper that empowers any data scientist to quickly train various deep learning models (text, vision, and many more). From version v0.8 onward, *ktrain* has also added support for *Hugging Face* transformers.

Using `text.Transformer()`, we first load the `distilbert-base-uncased_model` provided by *Hugging Face*:

```
import ktrain
from ktrain import text

model_name = 'distilbert-base-uncased'
t = text.Transformer(model_name, class_names=labels.unique(),
                     maxlen=500)
```

Once the model has been loaded, we use `t.preprocess_train()` and `t.prepro cess_test()` to process both the training and testing data:

```
train = t.preprocess_train(X_train_rus.tolist(), Y_train_rus.to_list())
```

When running the preceding code snippet on the training data, you will see the following output:

```
preprocessing train...
language: en
train sequence lengths:
        mean : 18
        95percentile : 34
        99percentile : 43
```

Similar to how we process the training data, we process the testing data as well:

```
val = t.preprocess_test(X_test_rus.tolist(), Y_test_rus.to_list())
```

When running the preceding code snippet on the training data, you will see the following output:

```
preprocessing test...
language: en
test sequence lengths:
        mean : 18
        95percentile : 34
        99percentile : 44
```

Once we have preprocessed both training and test datasets, we are ready to train the model. First, we retrieve the classifier and store it in the `model` variable.

In the BERT paper (*https://oreil.ly/j46Uy*), the authors selected the best fine-tuning hyperparameters from various batch sizes, including 8, 16, 32, 64, and 128; and learning rate ranging from 3e-4, 1e-4, 5e-5, and 3e-5, and trained the model for 4 epochs.

For this exercise, we use a `batch_size` of 8 and a learning rate of 3e-5, and trained for 3 epochs. These values are chosen based on common defaults used in many papers. The number of epochs was set to 3 to prevent overfitting:

```
model = t.get_classifier()
learner = ktrain.get_learner(model,
                      train_data=train,
                      val_data=val,
                      batch_size=8)

learner.fit_onecycle(3e-5, 3)
```

After you have run `fit_onecycle()`, you will observe the following output:

```
begin training using onecycle policy with max lr of 3e-05...
Train for 1027 steps, validate for 110 steps
Epoch 1/3
1027/1027 [==============================] - 1118s 1s/step -
loss: 0.6494 - accuracy: 0.6224 -
val_loss: 0.6207 - val_accuracy: 0.6527
Epoch 2/3
1027/1027 [==============================] - 1113s 1s/step -
loss: 0.5762 - accuracy: 0.6980 -
val_loss: 0.6039 - val_accuracy: 0.6695
Epoch 3/3
1027/1027 [==============================] - 1111s 1s/step -
loss: 0.3620 - accuracy: 0.8398 -
val_loss: 0.7672 - val_accuracy: 0.6567
<tensorflow.python.keras.callbacks.History at 0x7f309c747898>
```

Next, we evaluate the quality of the model by using `learner.validate()`:

```
learner.validate(class_names=t.get_classes())
```

The output shows the `precision`, `recall`, `f1-score`, and `support`:

```
              precision   recall  f1-score   support

           1       0.67     0.61      0.64      1752
           0       0.64     0.70      0.67      1752

    accuracy                          0.66      3504
   macro avg       0.66     0.66      0.66      3504
weighted avg       0.66     0.66      0.66      3504

array([[1069,  683],
       [ 520, 1232]])
```

ktrain enables you to easily view the top N rows where the model made mistakes. This enables one to quickly troubleshoot or learn more areas of improvement for the model. To get the top three rows where the model makes mistakes, use `learner.view_top_losses()`:

```
# show the top 3 rows where the model made mistakes
learner.view_top_losses(n=3, preproc=t)
```

This produces the following output:

```
id:2826 | loss:5.31 | true:0 | pred:1)


----------
id:3297 | loss:5.29 | true:0 | pred:1)


----------
id:1983 | loss:5.25 | true:0 | pred:1)
```

Once you have the identifier of the top three rows, let's examine one of the rows. As this is based on the quality of the weak labels, it is used as an example only. In a real-world case, you will need to leverage various data sources and subject-matter experts (SMEs) to deeply understand why the model has made a mistake in this area:

```
# Show the text  for the entry where we made mistakes
# We predicted 1, when this should be predicted as 0
print("Ground truth: %d" % Y_test_rus[2826])
print("-------------")
print(X_test_rus[2826])
```

The output is shown as follows: you can observe that even though the ground truth label is 0, the model has predicted it as a 1:

```
Ground truth: 1
-------------
"Tim Kaine announced he wants to raise taxes on everyone."
```

Using the Text Classification Model for Prediction

Let's use the trained model on a new instance of news, extracted from CNN News (*https://oreil.ly/sX0Sx*).

Using `ktrain.get_predictor()`, we first get the predictor. Next, we invoked `predictor.predict()` on news text. You will see how we obtain an output of 1:

```
news_txt = 'Now is a time for unity. We must \
respect the results of the U.S. presidential election and, \
as we have with every election, honor the decision of the voters \
and support a peaceful transition of power," said Jamie Dimon, \
CEO of JPMorgan Chase .'

predictor = ktrain.get_predictor(learner.model, preproc=t)
predictor.predict(news_txt)
```

ktrain also makes it easy to explain the results, using `predictor.explain()`:

```
predictor.explain(news_txt)
```

Running `predictor.explain()` shows the following output and the top features that contributed to the prediction:

```
y=0 (probability 0.023, score -3.760) top features

Contribution?    Feature
+0.783   of the
+0.533   transition
+0.456   the decision
+0.438   a time
+0.436   and as
+0.413   the results
+0.373   support a
+0.306   jamie dimon
+0.274   said jamie
+0.272   u s
+0.264   every election
+0.247   we have
+0.243   transition of
+0.226   the u
+0.217   now is
+0.205   is a
+0.198   results of
+0.195   the voters
+0.179   must respect
+0.167   election honor
+0.165   jpmorgan chase
+0.165   s presidential
+0.143   for unity
+0.124   support
+0.124   honor the
+0.104   respect the
+0.071   results
+0.066   decision of
+0.064   dimon ceo
+0.064   as we
+0.055   time for
-0.060   have
-0.074   power said
-0.086   said
-0.107   every
-0.115   voters and
-0.132   of jpmorgan
-0.192   must
-0.239   s
-0.247   now
-0.270   <BIAS>
-0.326   of power
-0.348   respect
```

```
-0.385  power
-0.394  u
-0.442  of
-0.491  presidential
-0.549  honor
-0.553  jpmorgan
-0.613  jamie
-0.622  dimon
-0.653  time
-0.708  a
-0.710  we
-0.731  peaceful
-1.078  the
-1.206  election
```

Finding a Good Learning Rate

It is important to find a good learning rate before you start training the model.

ktrain provides the lr_find() function for finding a good learning rate. lr_find() outputs the plot that shows the loss versus the learning rate (expressed in a logarithmic scale):

```
# Using lr_find to find a good learning rate
learner.lr_find(show_plot=True, max_epochs=5)
```

The output and plot (Figure 4-1) from running learner.lr_find() is shown next. In this example, you will see the loss value to be roughly in the range between 0.6 to 0.7. Once the learning rate gets closer to 10e-2, it increases significantly. As a general best practice, it is usually beneficial to choose a learning rate that is near the lowest point of the graph:

```
simulating training for different learning rates...this may take a few moments...
Train for 1026 steps
Epoch 1/5
1026/1026 [==============================] - 972s 947ms/step -
loss: 0.6876 - accuracy: 0.5356
Epoch 2/5
1026/1026 [==============================] - 965s 940ms/step -
loss: 0.6417 - accuracy: 0.6269
Epoch 3/5
1026/1026 [==============================] - 964s 939ms/step -
loss: 0.6968 - accuracy: 0.5126
Epoch 4/5
 368/1026 [=========>....................] - ETA: 10:13 - loss:
 1.0184 - accuracy: 0.5143

done.
Visually inspect loss plot and select learning rate associated with falling loss
```

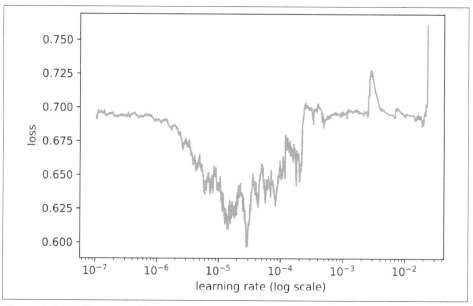

Figure 4-1. Finding a good learning rate using the visual plot of loss versus learning rate (log scale)

Using the output from `lr_find()`, and visually inspecting the loss plot as shown in Figure 4-1, you can start training the model using a learning rate, which has the least loss. This will enable you to get to a good start when training the model.

Using Hugging Face and Transformers

In the previous section, we showed how you can use *ktrain* to perform text classification. As you get familiar with using transformer-based models, you might want to leverage the full capabilities of the *Hugging Face* Python library directly.

In this section, we show you how you can use *Hugging Face* and one of the state-of-the-art transformers in *Hugging Face* called RoBERTa. RoBERTa uses an architecture similar to BERT and uses a byte-level BPE as a tokenizer. RoBERTa made several other optimizations to improve the BERT architecture. These include bigger batch size, longer training time, and using more diversified training data.

Loading the Relevant Python Packages

Let's start by loading the relevant *Hugging Face* Transformer libraries and *sklearn*.

In the code snippet, you will observe that we are loading several libraries. For example, we will be using `RobertaForSequenceClassification` and `RobertaTokenizer` for performing text classification and tokenization, respectively:

```
import numpy as np
import pandas as pd

from sklearn.preprocessing import LabelEncoder
from sklearn.linear_model import LogisticRegression
from sklearn.model_selection import cross_val_score
from sklearn.model_selection import train_test_split

import torch
import torch.nn as nn
import transformers as tfs

from transformers import AdamW, BertConfig
from transformers import RobertaTokenizer, RobertaForSequenceClassification
```

Dataset Preparation

Similar to the earlier sections, we will load the FakeNewsNet dataset. After we have loaded the `fakenews_df` DataFrame, we will extract the relevant columns that we will use to fine-tune the RoBERTa model:

```
# Read the FakeNewsNet dataset and show the first few rows
fakenews_df = pd.read_csv('../data/fakenews_snorkel_labels.csv')

X = fakenews_df.loc[:,['statement', 'snorkel_labels']]

# remove rows with a -1 snorkel_labels value
X = X[X['snorkel_labels'] >= 0]

labels = X.snorkel_labels
```

Next, we will split the data in *X* into the training, validation, and testing datasets. The training and validation dataset will be used when we train the model and do a model evaluation. The training, validation, and testing datasets are assigned to variables `X_train`, `X_val`, and `X_test`, respectively:

```
# Split the data into train/test datasets
X_train, X_test, y_train, y_test =
        train_test_split(X['statement'],
                         X['snorkel_labels'],
                         test_size=0.20,
                         random_state=122520)
```

```
# withold test cases for testing
X_test, X_val, y_test, y_val =
        train_test_split(X_test, y_test,
                        test_size=0.30,
                        random_state=122420)
```

Checking Whether GPU Hardware Is Available

In this section, we provide sample code to determine the number of available GPUs that can be used for training. In addition, we also print out the type of GPU:

```
if torch.cuda.is_available():
    device = torch.device("cuda")
    print(f'GPU(s) available: {torch.cuda.device_count()} ')
    print('Device:', torch.cuda.get_device_name(0))

else:
    device = torch.device("cpu")
    print('No GPUs available. Default to use CPU')
```

For example, running the preceding code on an Azure Standard NC6_Promo (6 vcpus, 56 GiB memory) Virtual Machine (VM), the following output is printed. The output will differ depending on the NVidia GPUs that are available on the machine that you are using for training:

```
GPU(s) available: 1
Device: Tesla K80
```

Performing Tokenization

Let's learn how you can perform tokenization using the RoBERTa tokenizer.

In the code shown, you will see that we first load the pretrained roberta-base model using RobertaForSequenceClassification.from_pretrained(...).

Next, we also loaded the pretrained tokenizer using RobertaTokenizer.from_pretrained(...):

```
model = RobertaForSequenceClassification.from_pretrained(
        'roberta-base',
        return_dict=True)

tokenizer = RobertaTokenizer.from_pretrained('roberta-base')
```

Next, you will use tokenizer() to prepare the training and validation data by performing tokenization, truncation, and padding of the data. The encoded training and validation data is stored in the variables tokenized_train and tokenized_validation, respectively.

We specify padding= *max_length* to control the padding that is used. In addition, we specify truncation=True to make sure we truncate the inputs to the maximum length specified:

```
max_length = 256

# Use the Tokenizer to tokenize and encode
tokenized_train = tokenizer(
    X_train.to_list(),
    padding='max_length',
    max_length = max_length,
    truncation=True,
    return_token_type_ids=False,
)

tokenized_validation = tokenizer(
    X_val.to_list(),
    padding='max_length',
    max_length = max_length,
    truncation=True,
    return_token_type_ids=False
)
```

 Hugging Face v3.x introduced new APIs for all tokenizers. See the documentation (*https://bit.ly/2VIqauj*) for how to migrate from v2.x to v3.x. In this chapter, we are using the new v3.x APIs for tokenization.

Next, we will convert the tokenized input_ids, attention mask, and labels into Tensors that we can use as inputs to training:

```
# Convert to Tensor
train_input_ids_tensor =
        torch.tensor(tokenized_train["input_ids"])

train_attention_mask_tensor =
        torch.tensor(tokenized_train["attention_mask"])

train_labels_tensor = torch.tensor(y_train.to_list())


val_input_ids_tensor =
        torch.tensor(tokenized_validation ["input_ids"])

val_attention_mask_tensor =
        torch.tensor(tokenized_validation ["attention_mask"])

val_labels_tensor = torch.tensor(y_val.to_list())
```

Model Training

Before we start to fine-tune the RoBERTa model, we'll create the DataLoader for both the training and validation data. The DataLoader will be used during the fine-tuning of the model. To do this, we first convert the `inputs_ids`, `attention_mask`, and `labels` to a `TensorDataset`. Next, we create the DataLoader using the TensorDataset as inputs and specify the batch size. We set the variable `batch_size` to be 16:

```
# Preparing the DataLaoders
from torch.utils.data import TensorDataset, DataLoader
from torch.utils.data import RandomSampler

# Specify a batch size of 16
batch_size = 16

# 1. Create a TensorDataset
# 2. Define the data sampling approach
# 3. Create the DataLoader
train_data_tensor = TensorDataset(train_input_ids_tensor,
            train_attention_mask_tensor,
            train_labels_tensor)

train_dataloader = DataLoader(train_data_tensor,
            batch_size=batch_size,
            shuffle=True)

val_data_tensor = TensorDataset(val_input_ids_tensor,
            val_attention_mask_tensor,
            val_labels_tensor)

val_dataloader = DataLoader(val_data_tensor,
            batch_size=batch_size,
            shuffle=True)
```

Next, we specify the number of epochs that will be used for fine-tuning the model and also compute the `total_steps` needed based on the number of epochs, and the number of batches in `train_dataloader`:

```
num_epocs = 2
total_steps = num_epocs * len(train_dataloader)
```

Next, we specify the optimizer that will be used. For this exercise, we will use the `AdamW` optimizer, which is part of the *Hugging Face* optimization module. The `AdamW` optimizer implements the Adam algorithm with the weight decay fix that can be used when fine-tuning models.

In addition, you will notice that we specified a scheduler, using `get_linear_sched ule_with_warmup()`. This creates a schedule with a learning rate that decreases linearly, using the initial learning rate that was set in the optimizer as the reference point. The learning rate decreases linearly after a warm-up period:

```
# Use the Hugging Face optimizer
from transformers import AdamW
from transformers import get_linear_schedule_with_warmup


optimizer = AdamW(model.parameters(), lr = 3e-5)

# Create the learning rate scheduler.
scheduler = get_linear_schedule_with_warmup(optimizer,
        num_warmup_steps = 100,
        num_training_steps = total_steps)
```

 The *Hugging Face* optimization module provides several optimiz-
ers, learning schedulers, and gradient accumulators. See this site
(*https://oreil.ly/9VFgX*) for how to use the different capabilities provided by the *Hugging Face* optimization module.

Now that we have the optimizer and scheduler created, we are ready to define the
fine-tuning training function called train(). First, we set the model to be in training
mode. Next, we iterate through each batch of data that is obtained from the
train_dataloader. We use optimizer.zero_grad() to clear previously calculated
gradients. Next, we invoke the forward pass with the model() function and retrieve
both the loss and logits after it completes. We add the loss obtained to the
total_loss and then invoke the backward pass by calling loss.backward().

To mitigate the exploding gradient problem, we clip the normalized gradiated to 1.0.
Next, we update the parameters using optimizer.step():

```
def train():
  total_loss = 0.0
  total_preds=[]

  # Set model to training mode
  model.train()

  # Iterate over the batch in dataloader
  for step,batch in enumerate(train_dataloader):
    # Get it batch to leverage device
    batch = [r.to(device) for r in batch]
    input_ids, mask, labels = batch

    model.zero_grad()
    outputs = model(input_ids,attention_mask=mask, labels=labels)

    loss = outputs.loss
    logits = outputs.logits

    # add on to the total loss
    total_loss = total_loss + loss
```

```
# backward pass
loss.backward()

# Reduce the effects of the exploding gradient problem
torch.nn.utils.clip_grad_norm_(model.parameters(), 1.0)

# update parameters
optimizer.step()

# Update the learning rate.
scheduler.step()

# append the model predictions
total_preds.append(outputs)

# compute the training loss of the epoch
avg_loss = total_loss / len(train_dataloader)



#returns the loss and predictions
return avg_loss
```

Similar to how we defined the fine-tuning function, we define the evaluation function, which is called evaluate(). We set the model to be in the evaluation model and iterate through each batch of data provided by val_dataloader. We used torch.no_grad() as we do not require the gradients during the evaluation of the model.

The average validation loss is computed once we have iterated through all the batches of validation data:

```
def evaluate():
  total_loss = 0.0
  total_preds = []

  # Set model to evaluation mode
  model.eval()

  # iterate over batches
  for step,batch in enumerate(val_dataloader):
    batch = [t.to(device) for t in batch]
    input_ids, mask, labels = batch

    # deactivate autograd
    with torch.no_grad():
      outputs = model(input_ids,attention_mask=mask, labels=labels)

      loss = outputs.loss
      logits = outputs.logits
```

```
    # add on to the total loss
    total_loss = total_loss + loss
    total_preds.append(outputs)

  # compute the validation loss of the epoch
  avg_loss = total_loss / len(val_dataloader)

  return avg_loss
```

Now that we have defined both the training and evaluation function, we are ready to start fine-tuning the model and performing an evaluation.

We first push the model to the available GPU and then iterate through multiple epochs. For each epoch, we invoke the `train()` and `evaluate()` functions and obtain both the training and validation loss.

Whenever we find a better validation loss, we will save the model to disk by invoking `torch.save()` and update the variable `best_val_loss`:

```
train_losses=[]
valid_losses=[]

# set initial loss to infinite
best_val_loss = float('inf')

# push the model to GPU
model = model.to(device)

# Specify the name of the saved weights file
saved_file = "fakenewsnlp-saved_weights.pt"

# for each epoch
for epoch in range(num_epocs):
    print('\n Epoch {:} / {:}'.format(epoch + 1, num_epocs))

    train_loss = train()
    val_loss = evaluate()

    print(f' Loss: {train_loss:.3f} - Val_Loss: {val_loss:.3f}')

    # save the best model
    if val_loss < best_val_loss:
        best_val_loss = val_loss
        torch.save(model.state_dict(),  saved_file)

    # Track the training/validation loss
    train_losses.append(train_loss)
    valid_losses.append(val_loss)

# Release the memory in GPU
model.cpu()
torch.cuda.empty_cache()
```

When we run the code, you will see the output with the training and validation loss for each epoch. In this example, the output terminates at epoch 2, and we have now a fine-tuned RoBERTa model using the data from the FakeNewsNet dataset:

```
Epoch 1 / 2
Loss: 0.649 - Val_Loss: 0.580

Epoch 2 / 2
Loss: 0.553 - Val_Loss: 0.546
```

Testing the Fine-Tuned Model

Let's run the fine-tuned RoBERTa model on the test dataset. Similar to how we prepared the training and validation datasets earlier, we will start by tokenizing the test data, performing truncation, and padding:

```
tokenized_test = tokenizer(
    X_test.to_list(),
    padding='max_length',
    max_length = max_length,
    truncation=True,
    return_token_type_ids=False
)
```

Next, we prepare the test_dataloader that we will use for testing:

```
test_input_ids_tensor = torch.tensor(tokenized_test["input_ids"])
test_attention_mask_tensor = torch.tensor(tokenized_test["attention_mask"])
test_labels_tensor = torch.tensor(y_test.to_list())

test_data_tensor = TensorDataset(test_input_ids_tensor,
                                 test_attention_mask_tensor,
                                 test_labels_tensor)

test_dataloader = DataLoader(test_data_tensor,
                             batch_size=batch_size,
                             shuffle=False)
```

We are now ready to test the fine-tuned RoBERTa model. To do this, we iterate through multiple batches of data provided by test_dataloader. To obtain the predicted label, we use torch.argmax() to get the label using the logits that are provided. The predicted results are then stored in the variable predictions:

```
total_preds = []
predictions = []

model = model.to(device)

# Set model to evaluation mode
model.eval()

# iterate over batches
```

```
for step,batch in enumerate(test_dataloader):
    batch = [t.to(device) for t in batch]
    input_ids, mask, labels = batch

    # deactivate autograd
    with torch.no_grad():
        outputs = model(input_ids,attention_mask=mask)
        logits = outputs.logits

        predictions.append(torch.argmax(logits, dim=1).tolist())
        total_preds.append(outputs)


model.cpu()
```

Now that we have the predicted results, we are ready to compute the performance metrics of the model. We will use `sklearn` classification report to get the different performance metrics for the evaluation:

```
from sklearn.metrics import classification_report

y_true = y_test.tolist()
y_pred = list(np.concatenate(predictions).flat)
print(classification_report(y_true, y_pred))
```

The output of running the code is shown:

```
              precision    recall  f1-score   support

           0       0.76      0.52      0.62       816
           1       0.66      0.85      0.74       885

    accuracy                           0.69      1701
   macro avg       0.71      0.69      0.68      1701
weighted avg       0.71      0.69      0.68      1701
```

Summary

Snorkel has been used in many real-world NLP applications across industry, medicine, and academia. At the same time, the field of NLP is evolving at a rapid pace. Transformer-based models have enabled many NLP tasks to be performed with high-quality results.

In this chapter, you learned how to use *Hugging Face* and *ktrain* to perform text classification for a FakeNewsNet dataset, which has been labeled by Snorkel in Chapter 3.

By combining the power of Snorkel for weak labeling and NLP libraries like *Hugging Face*, ML practitioners can get started with developing innovative NLP applications!

## CHAPTER 5

Using the Snorkel-Labeled Dataset for Image Classification

The techniques described in this chapter can be used for image classification for any image datasets. This chapter will provide you with a holistic set of discussions and code that can help you get started quickly with using the dataset that has been labeled by Snorkel (from Chapter 3).

The chapter starts with a gentle introduction to different types of visual object recognition tasks and discussions on how image features are represented. Next, we discuss how transfer learning for image classification works. In the remainder of the chapter, we will use the indoor/outdoor dataset that has been labeled by Snorkel to fine-tune an image classification model using PyTorch.

Visual Object Recognition Overview

Visual object recognition is commonly used to identify objects in digital images, and consists of one or more computer vision tasks:

Image classification
> Predict the type/class of an image (e.g., does the image consist of an indoor or outdoor scene?)

Object localization
> Identify the objects present in an image with bounding boxes

Object detection
> Identify the objects present in an image with bounding boxes and the type or class of the object corresponding to each bounding box

Image instance segmentation

Identify the objects present in an image and identify the pixels that belong to each of those objects

ImageNet is a visual database that consists of millions of images and is used by many computer vision (CV) researchers for various visual object recognition tasks. Convolutional neural networks (CNNs) are commonly used in visual object recognition. Over the years, researchers have continuously been advancing the performance of CNNs trained on ImageNet. In the early days of training AlexNet on ImageNet, it took several days to train the CNN. With innovations in algorithms and hardware, the time taken to train a CNN has decreased significantly.

For example, one type of CNN architecture is ResNet-50. ResNet-50 is a 50-layers-deep convolutional network that leverages residual networks. The model is trained to classify images into 1,000 object categories. Over the years, the time taken to train ResNet-50 on ImageNet from scratch has dropped from days to hours to minutes (shown in Table 5-1).

Table 5-1. Training ResNet-50 on ImageNet: how long does it take?

April 2017	Sept 2017	November 2017	July 2018	November 2018	March 2019
1 hour	31 minutes	15 minutes	6.6 minutes	2.0 minutes	1.2 minutes
Facebook, Caffe2	UC Berkeley, TACC, UC Davis, TensorFlow	Preferred Networks, ChainerMN	Tencent, TensorFlow	Sony, Neural Network Library (NNL)	Fujitsu, MXNet

In recent years, PyTorch and TensorFlow have been innovating at a rapid pace as powerful and flexible deep learning frameworks, empowering practitioners to easily get started with training CV and NLP deep learning models.

Model zoos provide AI practitioners with a large collection of deep learning models with pretrained weights and code. With the availability of model zoos with pretrained deep learning models, anyone can get started with any computer vision tasks (e.g., classification, object detection, image similarity, segmentation, and many more). This is amazing news for practitioners looking at leveraging some of these state-of-art CNNs for various computer vision tasks.

In this chapter, we will leverage ResNet-50 for classifying the images (indoor or outdoor scenes) that were labeled by Snorkel in Chapter 3.

Representing Image Features

In order to understand how image classification works, we need to understand how image features are represented in different layers of the CNN. One of the reasons why CNNs are able to perform well for image classification is because of the ability of the different layers of the CNN to extract the different salient features of an image (edges, textures) and group them as patterns and parts.

In the article "Feature Visualization," Olah, Mordvintsev, and Schubert[1] showed how each layer of a convolutional neural network (e.g., GoogLeNet) built up its understanding of edges, textures, patterns, and parts, and uses these basic constructs to build up the understanding of objects in an image (shown in Figure 5-1).

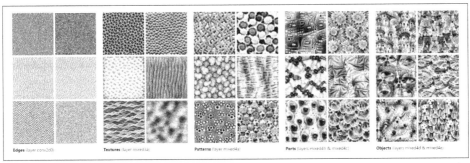

Figure 5-1. Feature visualization of different layers of GoogLeNet trained on ImageNet[2]

Transfer Learning for Computer Vision

Before the emergence of deep learning approaches for image classification, researchers working in computer vision (CV) leveraged and used various visual feature extractors to extract features that are used as inputs to classifiers. For example, histogram of oriented gradients (HoG) detectors are commonly used for feature extraction. Often, these custom CV approaches are not generalizable to new tasks (i.e., detectors trained for one image dataset are not easily transferrable to other datasets).

Today, many commercial AI applications that leverage computer vision capabilities use transfer learning. Transfer learning enables deep learning models that have been trained on large-scale image datasets (e.g., ImageNet) and uses the pretrained models for performing image classification, without having to train the models from scratch.[3]

1 Chris Olah, Alexander Mordvintsev, and Ludwig Schubert, "Feature Visualization," *Distill*, November 7, 2017, *https://distill.pub/2017/feature-visualization*.

2 Figure comes from Olah, Mordvintsev, and Schubert, "Feature Visualization."

3 Sebastian Ruder, "Transfer Learning - Machine Learning's Next Frontier," *Ruder* (blog), March 21, 2017, *https://ruder.io/transfer-learning*.

If you want to jump-start a deeper understanding of transfer learning and how to use CNNs for various visual recognition tasks, refer to the Stanford CS231n course "Convolutional Neural Networks for Visual Recognition" (*https://oreil.ly/f3n3a*).

There are several ways to use transfer learning for computer vision, including these two widely used approaches:

Using the CNN as a feature extractor
Each of the layers of a CNN encodes different features of the image. A CNN that has been trained on a large-scale image dataset would have captured these salient details in each of its layers. This enables the CNN to be used as a feature extractor and to extract the relevant feature inputs that can be used with an image classifier.

Fine-tuning the CNN
With a new image dataset, you might want to consider further fine-tuning the weights of the pretrained CNN model using backpropagation. As one moves from the top layers of a CNN to the last few layers, it is natural that the top layers capture generic image features (e.g., edges, textures, patterns, parts), and the later layers are tuned for a specific image dataset. By adjusting the weights of these last few layers of a CNN, the weights can be made more relevant to the image datasets. This process is called fine-tuning the CNN.

Now that we have a good overview of how CNNs are used for image classification, let's get started with building an image classifier for identifying whether an image shows an indoor or outdoor scene, using PyTorch.

Using PyTorch for Image Classification

In this section, we will learn how to use the pretrained ResNet-50 models—available in PyTorch—for performing image classification.

Before we get started, let's load the relevant Python libraries we will use in this chapter. These include common classes like `DataLoader` (which defines a Python iterable for datasets), `torchvision` and common utilities to load the pretrained CNN models, and image transformations that can be used.

We loaded `matplotlib` for visualization. In addition, we also used helper classes from *mpl_toolkits.axes_grid1*, which will enable us to display images from the training and testing datasets:

```
import torch
from torch.autograd import Variable
from torch.utils.data import DataLoader

import torchvision
from torchvision import datasets, models, transforms

import numpy as np
import os
import time
import copy

import matplotlib.pyplot as plt
from mpl_toolkits.axes_grid1 import ImageGrid

%matplotlib inline
```

Loading the Indoor/Outdoor Dataset

With the various Python libraries loaded, we are now ready to create the DataLoader objects on the indoor/outdoor images dataset. First, we specify the directory for loading the training, validation (i.e., val), and testing images. This is specified in the *data* directory:

```
# Specify image folder
image_dir = '../data/'

$ tree -d
.
├── test
│   ├── indoor
│   └── outdoor
├── train
│   ├── indoor
│   └── outdoor
└── val
    ├── indoor
    └── outdoor
```

Next, we specify the mean and standard deviation for each of the three channels for the images. These are defaults used for the ImageNet dataset and are generally applicable for most image datasets:

```
# Or we can use the default from ImageNet
mean = np.array([0.485, 0.456, 0.406])
std = np.array([0.229, 0.224, 0.225])
```

Computing the Mean and Standard Deviation for Your Dataset

You can compute the mean and standard deviation for all the images in the indoor/outdoor dataset as well. The following code snippet shown first loads the entire training set as one batch by using the `next()` function to return it. Once loaded, the mean and standard deviation for the training set is computed:

```
# Compute the mean and standard deviation of the image dataset
train_dataset = datasets.ImageFolder(
    os.path.join(image_dir, "train"),
    transform=transforms.Compose([transforms.Resize(224),
                                  transforms.CenterCrop(224),
                                  transforms.ToTensor()]))

loader = DataLoader(train_dataset,
    batch_size=len(train_dataset),
    num_workers=1)
    data = next(iter(loader))

mean, std = data[0].mean(), data[0].std()
```

You can use the computed values to replace the ImageNet mean and standard deviation values.

Next, we will specify the transformations that will be used for the training, validation, and testing datasets.

You will notice in the following code that for the training dataset, we first apply `RandomResizedCrop` and `RandomHorizontalFlip`. `RandomResizedCrop` crops each of the training images to a random size and then outputs an image that is 224 × 224. `RandomHorizontalFlip` randomly performs horizontal flipping of the 224 × 224 images. The image is then converted to tensor, and the tensor values are normalized to the mean and standard deviation provided.

For the validation and testing images, we resize each image to 224 × 224. Next, we perform a `CenterCrop`. The image is then converted to tensor, and the tensor values are normalized to the mean and standard deviation provided:

```
# Specify the image transformation
# for training, validation and testing datasets

image_transformations = {
    'train': transforms.Compose([
        transforms.RandomResizedCrop(224),
        transforms.RandomHorizontalFlip(),
        transforms.ToTensor(),
        transforms.Normalize(mean, std)
    ]),
```

```
    'val': transforms.Compose([
        transforms.Resize(224),
        transforms.CenterCrop(224),
        transforms.ToTensor(),
        transforms.Normalize(mean, std)
    ]),
        'test': transforms.Compose([
        transforms.Resize(224),
        transforms.CenterCrop(224),
        transforms.ToTensor(),
        transforms.Normalize(mean, std)
    ])
}
```

With the image transformations defined, we are now ready to create the Python itera-ble over the training, validation, and testing images using `DataLoader`. In the follow-ing code, we iterate through each folder (i.e., `train`, `val`, and `test`). For each of the folders, we specify the relative directory path and the image transformations.

Next, we define the `batch_size` as 8 and create a DataLoader object. We store the ref-erences for the training, validation, and testing loader in the `dataloders` variable so we can use it later. We also store the size of each dataset in the `dataset_sizes` variable:

```
# load the training,  validation, and test data
image_datasets = {}
dataset_sizes  = {}
dataloaders    = {}
batch_size     = 8

for data_folder in ['train', 'val', 'test']:
    dataset = datasets.ImageFolder(
                os.path.join(image_dir, data_folder),
                transform=image_transformations[data_folder])

    loader = torch.utils.data.DataLoader(dataset,
                                batch_size=batch_size,
                                shuffle=True,
                                num_workers=2)

    # store the dataset/loader/sizes for reference later
    image_datasets[data_folder] = dataset
    dataloaders[data_folder] = loader
    dataset_sizes[data_folder] = len(dataset)
```

Let's see the number of images in each of the datasets:

```
dataset_sizes
```

For this indoor and outdoor image classification exercise, we have 1,609, 247, and 188 images for training, validation, and testing, respectively:

```
{'train': 1609, 'val': 247, 'test': 188}
```

Let's see the class names for the datasets. This is picked up from the name of the directories stored in the data folder:

```
# Get the classes
class_names = image_datasets["train"].classes
class_names
```

You will see that we have two image classes: indoor and outdoor:

```
['indoor', 'outdoor']
```

Utility Functions

Next, let's define two utility functions (visualize_images and model_predictions), which will be used later for displaying the training and testing images and computing the predictions for the test dataset.

visualize_images() is a function for visualizing images in an image grid. By default, it shows 16 images from the images array. The array labels is passed to the function to show the class names for each of the images displayed. If the optional array predictions is provided, both the ground truth label and the predicted label will be shown side by side.

You will notice that we multiplied the value of inp by 255 and then cast it as a uint8 data type. This helps to convert the values from 0 to 1 to 0 to 255. It also helps to reduce the clipping errors that might occur due to negative values in the inp variable:

```
def visualize_images(images, labels, predictions=None,  num_images=16):

    count = 0
    mean = np.array([0.485, 0.456, 0.406])
    std = np.array([0.229, 0.224, 0.225])

    fig = plt.figure(1, figsize=(16, 16))
    grid = ImageGrid(fig, 111, nrows_ncols=(4, 4), axes_pad=0.05 )

    # get the predictions for data in dataloader
    for i in range(0,len(images)):
        ax = grid[count]

        inp = images[i].numpy().transpose((1, 2, 0))
        inp = std * inp + mean
        ax.imshow((inp * 255).astype(np.uint8))

        if (predictions is None):
          info = '{}'.format(class_names[labels[i]])
```

```
    else :
      info = '{}/{}'.format(class_names[labels[i]],
        class_names[predictions[i]])

    ax.text(10, 20, '{}'.format(info), color='w',
            backgroundcolor='black',
            alpha=0.8,
            size=15)

    count += 1
    if count == num_images:
      return
```

Given a DataLoader and a model, the function model_predictions() iterates through the images and computes the predicted label using the model provided. The predictions, ground truth labels, and images are then returned:

```
# given a dataloader, get the predictions using the model provided
def model_predictions(dataloder, model):
    predictions = []
    images = []
    label_list = []

    # get the predictions for data in dataloader
    for i, (inputs, labels) in enumerate(dataloder):
        inputs, labels = Variable(inputs.cuda()), Variable(labels.cuda())

        outputs = model(inputs)
        _, preds = torch.max(outputs.data, 1)

        predictions.append(preds.cpu())
        label_list.append(labels.cpu())

        for j in range(inputs.size()[0]):
            images.append(inputs.cpu().data[j])

    predictions_f = list(np.concatenate(predictions).flat)
    label_f = list(np.concatenate(label_list).flat)

    return predictions_f,  label_f, images
```

Visualizing the Training Data

It is important to have a deep understanding of the data before you start training the deep learning model. Let's use the visualize_images() function to show the first eight images in the training dataset (shown in Figure 5-2):

```
images, labels = next(iter(dataloaders['train']))
visualize_images(images, labels)
```

Figure 5-2. Training images for indoor and outdoor scene

Fine-Tuning the Pretrained Model

Many different kinds of pretrained deep learning model architectures can be used for image classification. PyTorch (and similarly, TensorFlow) provides a rich set of model architectures that you can use.

For example, in `TorchVision.Models` (*https://oreil.ly/CspHm*), you will see that PyTorch provides model definitions for AlexNet, VGG, ResNet, SqueezeNet, Dense-Net, Inception V3, GoogLeNet, ShuffleNet v2, MobileNet v2, ResNeXt, Wide ResNet, MNASNet, and more. Pretrained models are available by setting `pretrained=True` when loading the models.

For this exercise, we will use ResNet-50. We will load the pretrained ResNet-50 model and fine-tune it for the indoor/outdoor image classification task.

Residual Networks (or ResNet) was first introduced in the paper "Deep Residual Learning for Image Recognition" by Kaiming He et al.[4]

In the paper, the authors showed how residual networks can be easily optimized and explored with different network depths (up to 1,000 layers). In 2015, ResNet-based networks won first place in the ILSVRC classification task.

---

4 Kaiming He et al., "Deep Residual Learning for Image Recognition" (Preprint, submitted December 15, 2015), *https://arxiv.org/abs/1512.03385*.

Getting ready for training

First, we load the ResNet-50 model:

```
# Load Resnet50 model
model = models.resnet50(pretrained=True)
```

Resnet-50 is trained on ImageNet with 1,000 classes. We will need to update the fully connected (FC) layer to two classes:

```
# Specify a final layer with 2 classes - indoor and outdoor
num_classes = 2
num_features = model.fc.in_features
model.fc = torch.nn.Linear(num_features, num_classes)
```

Now that we have modified the FC layer, let's define the criterion, optimizer, and scheduler. We specify the loss function as Cross-EntropyLoss. The PyTorch Cross EntropyLoss() criterion combines both nn.LogSoftmax() and nn.NLLLoss() together and is commonly used for image classification problems with N classes.

For optimizer, torch.optim.SGD() is used. The stochastic gradient descent (SGD) optimization approach is commonly used in training CNN over batches of data.

For scheduler, lr_scheduler.StepLR() is used. The StepLR scheduler adjusts the learning rate by the value of gamma. In our example, we use the default gamma value of 0.1 and specified a step_size of 8:

```
import torch.optim as optim
from torch.optim import lr_scheduler

# Use CrossEntropyLoss as a loss function
loss_function = torch.nn.CrossEntropyLoss()

optimizer = torch.optim.SGD(model.fc.parameters(), lr=0.001, momentum=0.8)
scheduler = lr_scheduler.StepLR(optimizer, step_size=8)
```

We are ready to start fine-tuning the ResNet-50 model. Let's move the model to the GPU:

```
device = torch.device("cuda:0" if torch.cuda.is_available() else "cpu")
model.to(device)
```

When the model is moved to the GPU, it outputs the structure of the network. You will notice that the structure of the network reflects what is shown in Figure 5-3. In this chapter, we show a snippet of the network, and you can see the full network when you execute the code.

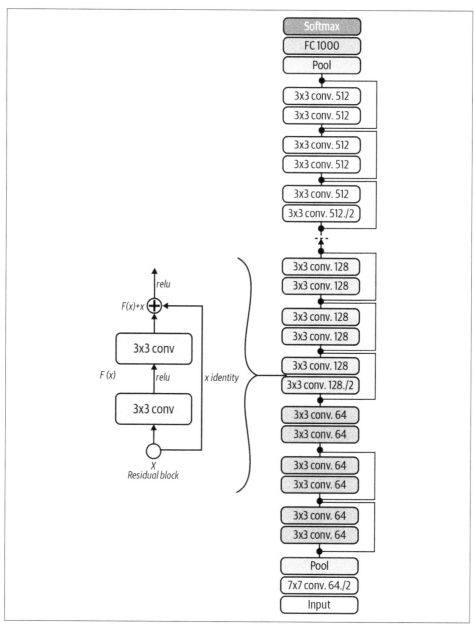

Figure 5-3. Architecture of ResNet, with different layers[5]

---

5 He et al., "Deep Residual Learning for Image Recognition."

In the PyTorch implementation of ResNet, you will see that the ResNet-50 implementation consists of multiple `Bottleneck` blocks, each with a kernel size of (1,1), (3,3), and (1,1). As noted in the TorchVision ResNet implementation (*https://oreil.ly/FBPZN*), the `Bottleneck` blocks used in TorchVision puts the stride for downsampling at 3 × 3 convolution.

In the last few layers of the ResNet-50 architecture, you will see the use of the 2D adaptive average pooling, followed by an FC layer that outputs two features (corresponding to the indoor and outdoor classes).

Now that the model has been pushed to the GPU, we are now ready to fine-tune the model with the training images of indoor and outdoor scenes:

```
ResNet(
  (conv1): Conv2d(3, 64, kernel_size=(7, 7), stride=(2, 2),
  padding=(3, 3), bias=False)
  (bn1): BatchNorm2d(64, eps=1e-05, momentum=0.1,
  affine=True, track_running_stats=True)
  (relu): ReLU(inplace=True)
  (maxpool): MaxPool2d(kernel_size=3, stride=2, padding=1,
  dilation=1, ceil_mode=False)
  (layer1): Sequential(
    (0): Bottleneck(
      (conv1): Conv2d(64, 64, kernel_size=(1, 1),
      stride=(1, 1), bias=False)
      (bn1): BatchNorm2d(64, eps=1e-05, momentum=0.1,
      affine=True, track_running_stats=True)
      (conv2): Conv2d(64, 64, kernel_size=(3, 3), stride=(1, 1),
      padding=(1, 1), bias=False)
      (bn2): BatchNorm2d(64, eps=1e-05, momentum=0.1,
      affine=True, track_running_stats=True)
      (conv3): Conv2d(64, 256, kernel_size=(1, 1),
      stride=(1, 1), bias=False)
      (bn3): BatchNorm2d(256, eps=1e-05, momentum=0.1,
      affine=True, track_running_stats=True)
      (relu): ReLU(inplace=True)
      (downsample): Sequential(
        (0): Conv2d(64, 256, kernel_size=(1, 1),
        stride=(1, 1), bias=False)
        (1): BatchNorm2d(256, eps=1e-05, momentum=0.1,
        affine=True, track_running_stats=True)
      )
    )
  )

  ... More layers ....

  )
  (avgpool): AdaptiveAvgPool2d(output_size=(1, 1))
  (fc): Linear(in_features=2048, out_features=2, bias=True)
)
```

The function `train()` (shown later in this section) is adapted from the example provided in the PyTorch tutorial "Transfer Learning for Computer Vision."[6]

We first perform a deep copy of all the pretrained model weights found in `model.state_dict()` and the variable `best_model_weights`. We initialize the best accuracy of the model to be 0.0.

The code then iterates through multiple epochs. For each epoch, we first load the data and labels that will be used for training and then push it to the GPU. We reset the optimizer gradient before calling `model(inputs)` to perform the forward pass. We compute the loss using `CrossEntropyLoss`. Once these steps are completed, we call `loss.backward()` for the backward pass. We then use `optimizer.step()` to update all the relevant parameters.

In the `train()` function, you will notice that we turn off the gradient calculation during the validation phase. This is because during the validation phase, gradient calculation is not required, and you simply want to use the validation inputs to compute the loss and accuracy only.

We checked whether the validation accuracy for the current epoch has improved over the previous epochs. If there are improvements in validation accuracy, we store the results in `best_model_weights` and set `best_accuracy` to denote the best validation accuracy observed so far:

```python
def train(model, criterion, optimizer, scheduler, num_epochs=10):
    # use to store the training and validation loss
    training_loss = []
    val_loss = []

    best_model_weights = copy.deepcopy(model.state_dict())
    best_accuracy = 0.0

    # Note the start time of the training
    start_time = time.time()

    for epoch in range(num_epochs):
        print('Epoch {}/{}, '.format(epoch+1, num_epochs), end = ' ' )

        # iterate through training and validation phase
        for phase in ['train', 'val']:

            total_loss = 0.0
            total_corrects = 0

            if phase == 'train':
```

---

6 Sasank Chilamkurthy, "Transfer Learning for Computer Vision Tutorial," PyTorch, accessed August 31, 2021, *https://pytorch.org/tutorials/beginner/transfer_learning_tutorial.html*.

```python
        model.train()
        print("[Training] ", end=' ')
    elif phase == 'val':
        model.eval()
        print("[Validation] ", end=' ')
    else:
        print("Not supported phase")

    for inputs, labels in dataloaders[phase]:
        inputs = inputs.to(device)
        labels = labels.to(device)

        # Reset the optimizer gradients
        optimizer.zero_grad()

        if phase == 'train':
            with torch.set_grad_enabled(True):
                outputs = model(inputs)
                _, preds = torch.max(outputs, 1)
                loss = criterion(outputs, labels)

                loss.backward()
                optimizer.step()
        else:
            with torch.set_grad_enabled(False):
                outputs = model(inputs)
                _, preds = torch.max(outputs, 1)
                loss = criterion(outputs, labels)

        total_loss += loss.item() * inputs.size(0)
        total_corrects += torch.sum(preds == labels.data)

    # compute loss and accuracy
    epoch_loss = total_loss / dataset_sizes[phase]
    epoch_accuracy =  (total_corrects + 0.0) / dataset_sizes[phase]

    if phase == 'train':
        scheduler.step()
        training_loss.append(epoch_loss)
    else:
        val_loss.append(epoch_loss)


    if phase == 'val' and epoch_accuracy > best_accuracy:
        best_accuracy = epoch_accuracy
        best_model_weights  = copy.deepcopy(model.state_dict())

    print('Loss: {:.3f} Accuracy: {:.3f}, '.format(
      epoch_loss, epoch_accuracy), end=' ')


print()
```

```
# Elapse time
time_elapsed = time.time() - start_time

print ('Train/Validation Duration: %s'
       % time.strftime("%H:%M:%S", time.gmtime(time_elapsed)))
print('Best Validation Accuracy: {:3f}'.format(best_accuracy))

# Load the best weights to the model
model.load_state_dict(best_model_weights )
return model, training_loss, val_loss
```

Fine-tuning the ResNet-50 model

Let's fine-tune the ResNet-50 model (with pretrained weights) using 25 epochs:

```
best_model, train_loss, val_loss = train(
                    model,
                    loss_function,
                    optimizer,
                    scheduler,
                    num_epochs=25)
```

From the output, you will see the training and validation loss over multiple epochs:

```
Epoch 1/25,
[Training]  Loss: 0.425 Accuracy: 0.796,
[Validation]  Loss: 0.258 Accuracy: 0.895,
Epoch 2/25,
[Training]  Loss: 0.377 Accuracy: 0.842,
[Validation]  Loss: 0.310 Accuracy: 0.891,
Epoch 3/25,
[Training]  Loss: 0.377 Accuracy: 0.837,
[Validation]  Loss: 0.225 Accuracy: 0.927,
Epoch 4/25,
[Training]  Loss: 0.357 Accuracy: 0.850,
[Validation]  Loss: 0.225 Accuracy: 0.931,
Epoch 5/25,
[Training]  Loss: 0.331 Accuracy: 0.861,
[Validation]  Loss: 0.228 Accuracy: 0.927,
...
Epoch 24/25,
[Training]  Loss: 0.302 Accuracy: 0.871,
[Validation]  Loss: 0.250 Accuracy: 0.907,
Epoch 25/25,
[Training]  Loss: 0.280 Accuracy: 0.886,
[Validation]  Loss: 0.213 Accuracy: 0.927,
Train/Validation Duration: 00:20:10
Best Validation Accuracy: 0.935223
```

After the model is trained, you will want to make sure that the model is not overfitting.

During the training of the model, we store the training and validation loss. This is returned by the train() function, and stored in the arrays train_loss and val_loss. Let's use this to plot the training and validation loss (shown in Figure 5-4), using the following code. From Figure 5-4, you will observe that the validation loss is consistently lower than the training loss. This is a good indication that the model has not overfitted the data:

```
# Visualize training and validation loss
num_epochs = 25

plt.figure(figsize=(9, 5))
plt.title("Training vs Validation Loss")
plt.xlabel("Epochs")
plt.ylabel("Loss")

plt.plot(range(1,num_epochs+1),train_loss,
         label="Training Loss",
         linewidth=3.5)

plt.plot(range(1,num_epochs+1),val_loss,
         label="Validation Loss",
         linewidth=3.5)

plt.ylim((0,1.))
plt.xticks(np.arange(1, num_epochs+1, 1.0))

plt.legend()
plt.show()
```

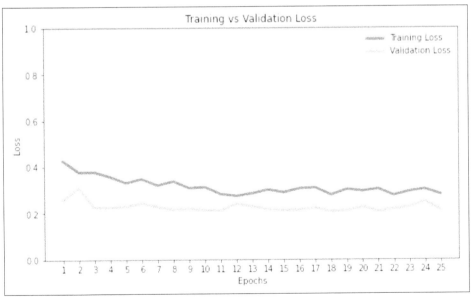

Figure 5-4. Training versus validation loss (number of epochs = 25)

There is definitely lots of room for further improvements to the model. For example, you can explore performing hyperparameter sweeps for the learning rate, momentum, and more.

Model evaluation

Now that we have identified the best model, let's use it to predict the class for the images in the test dataset. To do this, we use the utility function that we have defined earlier, model_predictions(). We provide as inputs the dataloader for the test dataset and the best model (i.e., best_model):

```
# Use the model for prediction using the test dataset
predictions, labels, images = model_predictions(dataloaders["test"],best_model)
```

Let's look at the classification report for the model using the test dataset:

```
# print out the classification report
from sklearn.metrics import classification_report
from sklearn.metrics import roc_auc_score

print(classification_report(labels, predictions))
print('ROC_AUC: %.4f' % (roc_auc_score(labels, predictions)))
```

The results are shown:

	precision	recall	f1-score	support
0	0.74	0.82	0.78	61
1	0.91	0.86	0.88	127
accuracy			0.85	188
macro avg	0.82	0.84	0.83	188
weighted avg	0.85	0.85	0.85	188

```
ROC_AUC: 0.8390
```

Let's visualize the ground truth and predicted labels for each of the test images. To do this, we use the utility function visualize_images() and pass as inputs: test images, labels, and predicted labels:

```
# Show the label, and prediction
visualize_images(images, labels, predictions )
```

The output of visualize_images() is shown in Figure 5-5.

Figure 5-5. Testing images for indoor and outdoor scenes; for each image, the ground truth labels are shown first, followed by the predicted labels

From Figure 5-5, you will see that the fine-tuned model is performing relatively well using the weak labels that have been produced by Snorkel in Chapter 3.

One of the images (shown on the second row, first image) is incorrectly classified. You will observe that this is a problem with the ground truth label and is not due to the image classifier that we have just trained. Snorkel has incorrectly labeled it as an outdoor image. In addition, you will notice that it is hard to tell whether the image is an indoor or outdoor image. Hence, the confusion.

Summary

In this chapter, you learned how to leverage the weakly labeled dataset generated using Snorkel to train a deep convolutional neural network for image classification in PyTorch. We also used concepts from transfer learning to incorporate powerful pre-trained computer vision models into our model training approach.

While the indoor-outdoor application discussed here is relatively simple, Snorkel has been used to power a broad set of real-world applications in computer vision ranging from medical image interpretation to scene graph prediction. The same principles outlined in this chapter on using Snorkel to build a weakly supervised dataset for a new modality can be extended to other domains like volumetric imaging (e.g., computed tomography), time series, and video.

It is also common to have signals from multiple modalities at once. This cross-modal setting described by Dunnmon et al.[7] represents a particularly powerful way to combine the material from Chapters 4 and 5. In brief, it is common to have image data that is accompanied by free text (clinical report, article, caption, etc.) describing that image. In this setting, one can write labeling functions over the text and ultimately use the generated labels to train a neural network over the associated image, which can often be easier than writing labeling functions over the image directly.

There exists a wide variety of real-world situations in which this cross-modal weak supervision approach can be useful because we have multiple modalities associated with any given data point, and the modality we wish to operate on at test time is harder to write labeling functions over than another we may have available at training time. We encourage the reader to consider a cross-modal approach when planning how to approach building models for a particular application.

Transfer learning for both computer vision (discussed in this chapter) and natural language processing (NLP) (discussed in Chapter 4) has enabled data scientists and researchers to effectively transfer the knowledge learned from large-scale datasets and adapt it to new domains. The availability of pretrained models for both computer vision and NLP has drove rapid innovations in the machine learning/deep learning community, and we encourage the reader to consider how transfer learning can be combined with weak supervision wherever possible.

Going forward, we expect that the powerful combination of Snorkel and transfer learning will create a flywheel that drives AI innovations and success in both commercial and academic settings.

---

7 Jared Dunnmon et al., "Cross-Modal Data Programming Enables Rapid Medical Machine Learning Patterns" (Preprint, submitted March 26, 2019), *https://arxiv.org/abs/1903.11101*.

## CHAPTER 6

Scalability and Distributed Training

The examples that we have seen in the previous chapters are considered toy examples and relatively simple. They can fit and run in the memory and compute constraints of a single machine. Most enterprises have larger datasets and more complex requirements that need to scale bigger than one machine. In this chapter, we will look at architecture and techniques that will help enterprises scale Snorkel.

When we think about scaling Snorkel, we essentially are looking to run labeling functions distributed across several machines, typically as part of a cluster.

In this chapter, we will start by exploring Apache Spark as the core set of technologies that allow us to scale Snorkel. Instead of custom engineering a solution that would need to factor in the infrastructure and plumbing needed to scale, Apache Spark can do this out of the box and is already a popular option when it comes to big data and production deployments within enterprises.

We will use the NLP-based fake news example from Chapter 3 and see how we can scale it with Apache Spark. During this journey, we will understand the code and design changes that are needed to allow us to achieve a fake news implementation that we can distribute and deploy at a massive scale.

Bigger models create pressure on the underlying systems for training and inference, which is where we learn from the experience of other well-established software engineering paradigms of high-performance computing (HPC) and web-scale architecture.

HPC is the study and use of very fast supercomputers using parallel processing techniques and running on multiple nodes. This allows for solving complex computational challenges. HPC typically would include both the engineering and the operational aspects to build, deploy, and manage these instances. We will touch on some of these system architectures but leave the details as an exercise for you to explore.

Before we get into details of Apache Spark and explore how we can use that to help scale Snorkel, let's discuss the need for scalability and distributed training.

The Need for Scalability

Weak supervision enables ML practitioners to generate massive training datasets and, in turn, build better ML and higher-quality ML models. Model training routines, therefore, need to be able to scale to incorporate and handle as much training data as possible. As outlined in Chapter 1, the memory and compute resource requirements to programmatically label and train models on massive training sets mean the data cannot fit on one machine. In other words, some kind of scaling is needed. Commonly for scaling, there are two options—horizontal and vertical scaling, as shown in Figure 6-1.

Vertical scaling (also known as scaling up) is adding more hardware to existing infrastructure, often using a more powerful machine than the one we might be using right now, allowing the system to handle more load. Scaling up will work for some time until you hit the largest machine available on your platform. Currently, most public cloud providers offer single servers with up to 120 virtual CPUs and 448 GBs of RAM (such as Azure's HBv3-series (*https://oreil.ly/7hGhp*)).

Horizontal scaling, or scaling out, is adding new machines (i.e., nodes) to the infrastructure allowing the system to handle more load by distributing the additional load across a number of these nodes, typically managed as part of a cluster. For highly parallelizable workloads like applying labeling functions to a partitioned dataset, there is almost no limit to scaling horizontally as you can continue adding commodity servers as compute nodes.

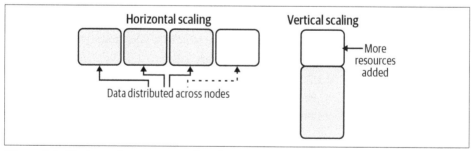

Figure 6-1. Horizontal versus vertical scaling

When scaling out big data workloads, we have two sets of layers—the storage layer and the compute layer. While in principle, both these layers don't have to be interdependent, they are practically correlated and need to be considered in the context of each other.

The storage layer deals with the actual distributed storage (or distributed file system) and associated I/O constraints and trade-offs across multiple nodes and subsystems. The compute layer, on the other hand, is where data is processed when loaded. When scaling weak supervision, both of these layers become critical and possibly contention points.

In the context of machine learning, the scalability attributes between training and prediction (i.e., inference) are often different. For training, typically we need to load the entire training data in memory, making vertical scaling the simplest option.

For inference, on the other hand, we only need batches of data instances loaded at a time. Modern frameworks support distributed training routines and training on streaming datasets, making it possible to train on horizontally scaled architectures at the cost of infrastructural complexity. We take a closer look in the next section.

Distributed Training

In distributed training, the workload to train a model is split up and shared among multiple nodes (i.e., machines) called worker nodes. These worker nodes work in parallel to speed up model training.

Distributed training can be used for traditional ML models but is better suited for compute and time-intensive tasks, like training deep neural networks, data programming, and generating weak labels.

Applying labeling functions to large datasets lends itself naturally to horizontally scaled infrastructure. Each labeling function runs independently of the other, with the output collated back.

There are two fundamental approaches—data parallelism and model parallelism:

Data parallelism
> For a compute cluster, the data is divided into chunks (i.e., partitions) that are correlated with the available worker nodes in that cluster. Each node gets a copy of the model and operates on its subset of the data and computes its predictions and errors. To get a consistent single model, the parameters and gradients from each node need to be synchronized across the cluster.

Model parallelism

Different segments of a model run in parallel on different nodes, and each operates on the same data. It is important to note that the models are being evaluated concurrently, and the order of evaluation should not matter. The algorithm's ability to parallelize tasks dictates the scalability of this approach. Fundamentally, model parallelism is more complex to implement than data parallelism.

 We cannot think about model parallelism without understanding the details of parallel algorithms and parallel programming. Each of these topics is complex in its own right, with books written on the subject, and getting into details of these topics is outside the scope of this book.

In addition, to avoid confusion and keep to the topic of weak supervision, we also do not outline hybrid parallelism, where we combine the different schemes of data and model parallelism and try and get the best of both worlds.

"Demystifying Parallel and Distributed Deep Learning,"[1] "Integrated Model, Batch and Domain Parallelism in Training Neural Networks,"[2] and "Efficient Large-Scale Language Model Training on GPU Clusters"[3] are some of the suggested reading material for readers who are curious about the details on these topics when thinking about distributed training and parallelism.

In this chapter, we will focus on data parallelism. We will use Apache Spark as the runtime that allows us to implement data parallelism. To do this, we need to understand a little bit of Spark's design principles and architecture. In the next section, we will look at Apache Spark and how the Spark runtime can help us scale weak supervision within an enterprise.

---

1 Tal Ben-Nun and Torsten Hoefler, "Demystifying Parallel and Distributed Deep Learning: An In-Depth Concurrency Analysis" (Preprint, submitted September 15, 2018), *https://arxiv.org/pdf/1802.09941*.

2 Amir Gholami et al., "Integrated Model, Batch and Domain Parallelism in Training Neural Networks" (Preprint, submitted May 16, 2018), *https://arxiv.org/abs/1712.04432*.

3 Deepak Narayanan et al., "Efficient Large-Scale Language Model Training on GPU Clusters Using Megatron-LM" (Preprint, submitted August 15, 2021), *https://arxiv.org/pdf/2104.04473*.

Apache Spark: An Introduction

Apache Spark (*http://spark.apache.org*) is a unified analytics engine for large-scale compute and data processing, which can be deployed both on premises or in the cloud. Spark[4] was inspired by Google's MapReduce implementation,[5] and while it is designed for large-scale data processing, it has been extended to support streaming and real-time implementations.

Apache Spark is an ideal runtime for scaling up data programming and ML, as it provides in-memory storage for intermediate computations and a composable API design. This composable API design allows us to incorporate different ML libraries and interact with real-time data and graph processing engines.

Spark has the following four principles that form the cornerstone of weak supervision scalability design:

Speed

> Spark features in-memory implementation and optimization across multiple cores and efficient parallel processing, multithreading, and query optimization based on a directed acyclic graph (DAG).

Ease of use

> Spark is easy to use, as it abstracts out all the complexities of distributed computing into a logical data structure called resilient distributed dataset (RDD). The RDD is an immutable distributed collection, where each object has a set of operations that support transformations and actions. The RDD is implemented across different programming languages and other higher-level data structures such as DataFrames and datasets.

Modularity

> Spark supports different programming languages and workloads that can be used consistently across these languages. One doesn't need to switch programming languages or learn new APIs specific to a workload since the unified processing engine brings it together across SQL, R, Python, Java, and Scala, to name a few.

4 Matei Zaharia et al., "Apache Spark: A Unified Engine for Big Data Processing," *Communications of the ACM* 59, no. 11 (November 2016): 56–65, *https://dl.acm.org/doi/10.1145/2934664*.

5 Jeffrey Dean and Sanjay Ghemawat, "MapReduce: Simplified Data Processing on Large Clusters," in *OSDI'04: Sixth Symposium on Operating System Design and Implementation* (Operating Systems Design and Implementation Conference, San Francisco, CA, 2004), 137–150, accessed August 18, 2021, *https://research.google/pubs/pub62*.

Extensibility

Spark decouples the storage and computer and focuses on the fast parallel computation engine. This decoupling allows for a rich ecosystem of third-party packages, supporting a myriad of different data sources from traditional RDBMS, Hadoop, MongoDB, Cassandra, etc., and the more recent cloud storage abstractions such as Azure Storage, AWS S3, Kinesis, etc. This extensibility is very helpful, and when using Snorkel, we are writing labeling functions that incorporate varied unstructured data sources.

Unsurprisingly, Spark has become a popular choice among enterprises and developers who operate with big data. It not only allows us to tackle large datasets, but does all of this using the programming language and APIs that are familiar to many.

> Going deep with Apache Spark is outside the scope of this book. If you are interested in more details with Spark's application stack and runtime, the authors of this book can highly recommend *Learning Spark*, 2nd Edition (O'Reilly) (*https://oreil.ly/10PRC*) by Jules Damji et al., having used it in a personal capacity.

At a high level, a typical Spark application stack has four distinct components (see the first row of Figure 6-2) that support the design principles outlined earlier and support the core features that we use when writing a Spark application. The APIs exposed via these components get converted into a DAG that is executed by the core engine.

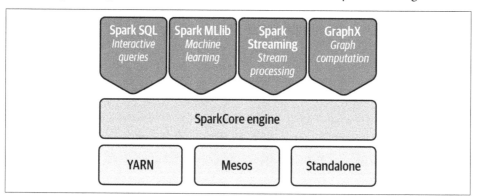

Figure 6-2. Spark stack

As we think about designing labeling functions with Snorkel, we need to be aware of Spark's application constraint and runtime. In the next section, we will look at Spark's runtime and application design—and how we can deploy and use it to scale.

Spark Application Design

Spark can run by itself, on one machine, or on several machines as part of a cluster. A Spark application can run independently on one machine or as part of a cluster. Spark has an out-of-the-box feature to manage clusters and also has the support to plug in other types of cluster managers such as YARN, Mesos, etc. The Spark application invokes a spark session (called a `SparkSession`) using a Spark driver.

For any Spark application, the main entry point for execution is via the Spark driver. As shown in Figure 6-3, the Spark driver is responsible for all communication with the cluster—from requesting more resources to executing operations on nodes. The `SparkSession`, in effect, is the unified conduit to all of the data and operations that Spark supports.

`SparkSession` coordinates and transforms all the operations into underlying computations, and it distributes and schedules those as tasks across the different nodes on the cluster. In this process, the `SparkSession` is using the cluster manager to request the relevant resources (such as memory, CPU, etc.) needed.

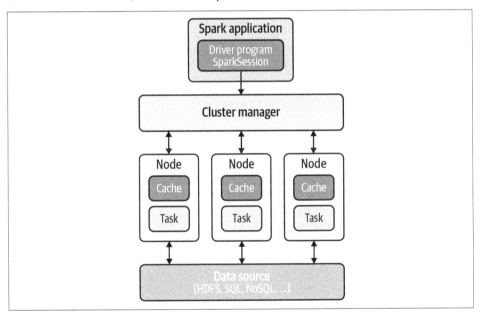

Figure 6-3. Spark application architecture

As we called out earlier in this chapter, we will use the NLP-based fake news example from Chapter 3 and deploy that on Spark. And during that process, we will understand the design changes and implementation that allow us to run at scale.

We could deploy a cluster of many machines and configure Apache Spark (and the relevant clusters, networks, etc.), but that would take time and management resources. Instead, we opt to use a cloud instance of Spark running on Azure Databricks.

Databricks Versus Apache Spark

Apache Spark is an open source distributed computing framework that is built on Scala and came out of the University of California, Berkeley.

Databricks is a company founded by the original creators of Apache Spark and is a commercial offering that adds additional features that are part of the paid offering. Databricks also has cloud-hosted options that make it very easy for most to start.

For a more detailed comparison between the two options, see the Spark and Databricks comparison (*https://oreil.ly/UFgFj*).

In the next section, we will see how to set up Azure Databricks as our runtime and instance to deploy our example and show how we can scale Snorkel.

Using Azure Databricks to Scale

Azure Databricks is a cloud-hosted platform of Databricks that is integrated with the rest of Azure and that supports one-click deployments and a Databricks dashboard, as shown in Figure 6-4.

Using a hosted Databricks implementation helps us concentrate more on the task at hand of scaling Snorkel and weak supervision and less on the technical aspects of the cluster, nodes, network, security, etc. All of these are critical but are something we cannot discuss in the context of this book.

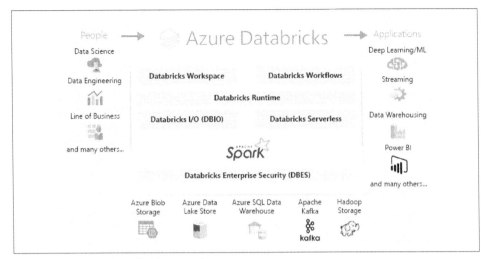

Figure 6-4. Azure Databricks overview

Databricks is one of the options that we have out of the box to deploy on Azure. On the one hand, deploying a new instance of Databricks using the Azure portal is quite straightforward, as Figure 6-5 shows. On the other hand, there are several steps and much preparatory work needed to configure Databricks before we can use it for Snorkel.

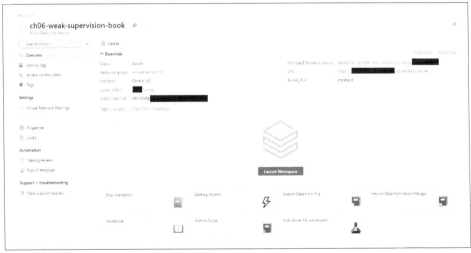

Figure 6-5. Azure Databricks deployment

To deploy our instance, all we need is an active Azure subscription. The quickstart guide (*https://oreil.ly/GovW1*) shows a detailed step-by-step instruction on how to deploy and get going with Databricks on Azure.

Cloud Options for Databricks

From our perspective, we are using Azure more for convenience, but other cloud providers would work. In addition to Azure, Databricks has other cloud-hosted options from the major cloud providers, including AWS, Google, and Alibaba. All of these allow you to deploy, manage, and scale a data platform securely and conveniently.

Once deployed, we will use the Databricks workspace, as shown in Figure 6-6. This workspace is our entry point to Databricks and something we will use for most of our interactions with Databricks. In this interface, we will create a new Jupyter Notebook (or import one from the book GitHub repository (*https://bit.ly/WeakSupervision Book*)), spin up a new cluster to run our code, and set up different jobs to automate, among other things.

Detailed and specific configuration options for Azure Databricks are beyond the scope of this book. If Databricks is new to you, it is recommended that you read the Azure Databricks documentation (*https://oreil.ly/l116i*) for details and best practices.

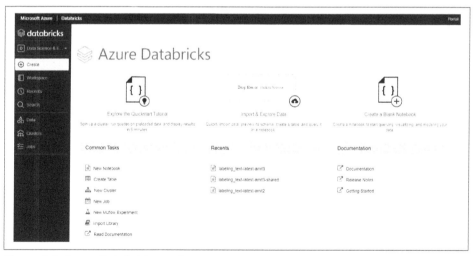

Figure 6-6. Azure Databricks workspace

Cluster Setup for Weak Supervision

First, we need to configure a cluster. When configuring the cluster, in addition to node details we also need to outline the packages and related dependencies that need to be deployed on each node. As part of the cluster configuration, we need to choose the Databricks runtime version, a cluster policy, and behavior at runtime.

Figure 6-7 shows the configuration that we are using to run Snorkel and what we will use when labeling the FakeNewsNet dataset from Chapter 3.

For more details on all the configuration options on Azure Databricks, see the cluster configuration articles (*https://oreil.ly/5RpOe*).

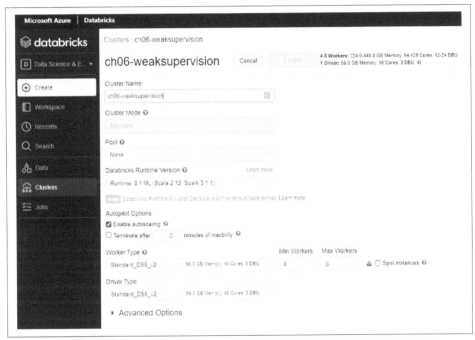

Figure 6-7. Azure Databricks cluster configuration

Cluster configuration

For us to be able to run and label the FakeNewsNet dataset on Spark, there are a few dependencies that are needed. As outlined earlier in the chapter, for a cluster to be able to scale up and down, these dependencies need to be consistent across all nodes.

To get our deployment on Spark, we will configure the libraries in the following list. This configuration is effectively the same when we do a `pip install` on a single machine that will install the latest versions available. If there is a dependency on a specific version, that can be outlined as shown in "TensorFlow Library" on page 142:

- `nltk`
- `snorkel`
- `tldextract`
- `bs4`
- `elephas`
- `keras`

To install these specific libraries for the cluster, in the Libraries option we choose PyPI and enter the package name as shown in Figure 6-8. In our case, all of these are available in the default PiPI index, and we don't need a specific repository.

Figure 6-8. Library installation for the cluster

Figure 6-9 shows the status of libraries for the cluster once everything is installed and ready to use.

Be aware that the GUI does not validate the libraries for either compatibility or correctness. So, if there are any typos or incompatibilities, the library installer will try to install those incompatible or incorrect libraries and it will eventually fail. This can have an impact on the availability of some of the nodes as they get spun up.

TensorFlow Library

In some cases, we had to explicitly install TensorFlow, even though this was already part of Databricks runtime and should not be explicitly required. The following example installs the CPU-optimized version 2.4 of TensorFlow on the cluster:

```
tensorflow-cpu==2.4.*
```

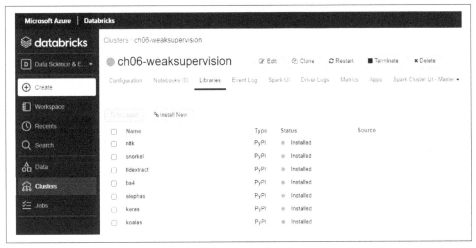

Figure 6-9. Library installation for the cluster

Fake News Detection Dataset on Databricks

Back in Chapter 3, we set up the fake news detection (FakeNewsNet) as an example that we go running end to end on a single machine. Now, we'll see how we can scale FakeNewsNet from one machine to a cluster running Databricks.

As a reminder, the fake news detection dataset contains three files: train, validation, and test. We are only using the training file (*fnn_train.csv*). At the time of writing, this file contains 15,212 records, and while this is labeled data, we will be ignoring that and treating it as if it wasn't.

The FakeNewsNet dataset contains the columns in Table 6-1.

Table 6-1. FNN columns

Columns	Description
id	An identifier for each sample, representing the PolitiFact website ID for this article
date	The time of publishing
speaker	The person or organization to whom this statement is attributed
statement	The claim published by the speaker
sources	The sources that have been used to analyze each statement
paragraph_based_content	Paragraph from where the statement is taken
fullText_based_content	Full text from where the paragraph got extracted

We will also be using the fake news detection (LIAR) dataset from earlier. This dataset is collected by crawling PolitiFact. The labels used for the claims are from the six ratings in Truth-O-Meter, as shown in Table 6-2.

Table 6-2. Truth-O-Meter ratings

Rating	Description
TRUE	Statement is true.
MOSTLY TRUE	Statement is accurate but needs additional clarification.
HALF TRUE	Statement is only partially accurate.
MOSTLY FALSE	Statement ignores facts that might create a different impression.
FALSE	Statement is mostly inaccurate.
PANTS ON FIRE	Statement is inaccurate.

From a dataset perspective, the changes that are needed are minimal and we can reuse most things. Given that we are not running this locally, we need to upload the FakeNewsNet and LIAR datasets to the Databricks cluster.

In Spark, there are many ways to connect to different data sources. In our case, we will upload the data to the cluster using the GUI option that Spark offers, as shown in Figure 6-10.

If you don't see the GUI option to upload the data, this is a setting that needs to be enabled in the advanced settings as part of the Admin console. See file upload interface documentation (*https://oreil.ly/62PjO*) for details.

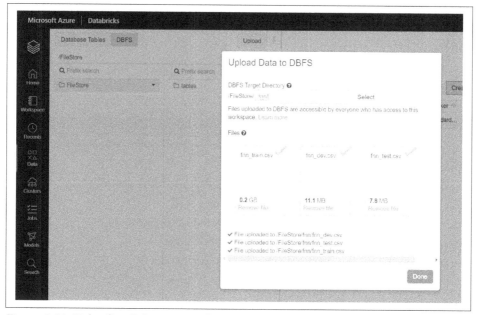

Figure 6-10. Uploading FakeNewsNet (FNN) data to Databricks

We upload both the LIAR and the FNN datasets in their respective folders. Once completed, we should see the data available to load in the cluster, as shown in Figure 6-11.

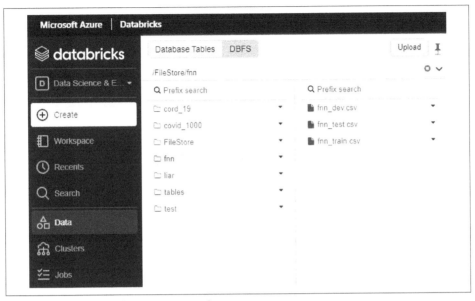

Figure 6-11. FNN and LIAR training data

Labeling Functions for Snorkel

When it comes to the labeling functions themselves, we see there is no change from earlier to run them at scale with Spark. We also see the options that the classifiers will use to abstain remain the same:

```
ABSTAIN = -1
FAKE = 0
REAL = 1
```

Table 6-3 outlines the labeling functions from earlier that we will reuse.

Table 6-3. The labeling functions

Labeling Function	Comment
label_rp()	Crowdsourcing from RealClear politics
label_wp()	Crowdsourcing using Washington Post
label_gb()	Crowdsourcing from Glenn Beck
label_snopes()	Snopes—Fact-check ratings
label_politifact()	PolitiFact
factcheckqa()	FactCheck.org

Labeling Function	Comment
factcheckafpqa()	AFP Fact Check
speaker()	Transfer learning with LIAR dataset

As a reminder, the `factcheckqa()` and `factcheckafpqa()` functions check FactCheck or AFP Fact Check sentiment score, respectively, and return REAL if the sentiments are mostly positive, FAKE if the sentiments are mostly negative, and ABSTAIN if otherwise:

```
def factcheck_sentiment(row, columnName):
    label = str(row[columnName])
    score = 0
    if(label):
        claims = label[1:-1].split(',')
        for claim in claims:
            print(claim)
            sentiment = sid.polarity_scores(claim)
            print(sentiment)
            if(sentiment["neg"] > sentiment["pos"]):
                score -=1
            elif(sentiment["pos"] > sentiment["neg"]):
                score +=1
        if(score > 0):
            return REAL
        elif (score < 0):
            return FAKE
        else:
            return ABSTAIN
    return ABSTAIN

@labeling_function()
def factcheckqa_sentiment(row):
    return factcheck_sentiment(row, "www.factcheck.org")

@labeling_function()
def factcheckafpqa_sentiment(row):
    return factcheck_sentiment(row, "factcheck.afp.com")

@labeling_function()
def label_snopes(row):
    label = str(row["www.snopes.com"])
    if label is not None:
        if ('real' in label):
            return REAL
        else:
            return FAKE
    else:
        return ABSTAIN

truth_o_meter = {
    "true": 4,
```

```
        "mostly-true": 3,
        "half-true": 2,
        "barely-true": 1,
        "mostly-false": -1,
        "false": -2,
        "pants-fire": -3
    }

    @labeling_function()
    def label_politifact(row):
        total_score = 0
        labels = row["www.politifact.com"]
        if(labels):
            labels = str(row["www.politifact.com"]).split(',')
            # The last label has the newline character
            if(len(labels) > 0):
                labels[-1] = labels[-1][:-2]
            for label in labels:
                label = label.strip()
                if(label in truth_o_meter):
                    total_score += truth_o_meter[label]
        if(total_score > 0):
            return REAL
        if(total_score < 0):
            return FAKE

        return ABSTAIN
```

Setting Up Dependencies

The first thing we need to do is set up dependencies, including the packages needed. These are mostly the same from earlier, with a few exceptions needed in the Databricks runtime:

```
import pandas as pd
import nltk
import collections
import itertools
from collections import Counter
import tldextract
import numpy as np

# web
from urllib.request import Request, urlopen
from bs4 import BeautifulSoup
import time
import JSON
```

We also import the snorkel packages that are needed. The one difference we have is the use of SparkLFApplier, which is part of Snorkel's labeling package and expects a Spark RDD as input. Unlike a Pandas DataFrame that is designed to run on one machine, a Spark RDD is designed to run on a cluster comprising of many nodes, allowing it to scale:

```
# snorkel
from snorkel.labeling import labeling_function
from snorkel.labeling.apply.spark import SparkLFApplier
from snorkel.labeling.model import MajorityLabelVoter
from snorkel.labeling import LFAnalysis
from snorkel.labeling.model import LabelModel
```

We also set up and initialize variables and sentiment analysis, which is used by the fact-checking functions later:

```
# data filenames
TRAINING_dataFile = "/dbfs/FileStore/fnn/fnn_train.csv"

## training dataset
WORKING_dataFile = "/dbfs/FileStore/test/working_fnn_train.csv"
WORKING2_dataFile = "/dbfs/FileStore/test/working_processed_fnn_train.csv"
CLEANED_dataFile = "/dbfs/FileStore/test/working_processed_fnn_train_clean.csv"

TRAINED_dataFile = "/dbfs/FileStore/test/data_nlp.csv"

# Load the Liar dataset
LIAR_dataFile = "/dbfs/FileStore/liar/liar_train.csv" #training dataset
```

We also initialize the sentiment analysis package, which is used by some of the labeling functions:

```
#In some cases a call later will fail, and this is needed on Apache Spark
from nltk.corpus import stopwords
from nltk.stem import WordNetLemmatizer
from nltk.sentiment.vader import SentimentIntensityAnalyzer

nltk.download('vader_lexicon')
sid = SentimentIntensityAnalyzer()
```

Spark Dataframes Versus Pandas DataFrames

In addition to RDDs (outlined earlier in this chapter), Spark also has a set of DataFrame APIs that are an extension to the RDD APIs. DataFrames represent data in a tabular fashion and are conceptually equivalent to a table in an RDMS, a DataFrame in Python, or an Excel spreadsheet. For those using Pandas, these DataFrame APIs would seem similar.

However, under the covers, both are quite different, and this similarity can be quite deceiving. Pandas DataFrames are designed to work on one machine and with the constraints of memory and compute of that machine. On the other hand, a Spark DataFrame is a distributed representation designed to scale across large clusters with petabytes of data and implements vastly different code generation and optimization techniques.

Pandas DataFrame employs an eager execution, with the code executed immediately; Spark DataFrames, on the other hand, implement a lazy execution system and don't execute until needed. This results in vastly different behaviors. For example, with Pandas DataFrames, the data is mutable, while with Spark DataFrames, the data is immutable. In Pandas we can use the `'[]'` operator, but in Spark we need to use the `.withColumn()` method.

It is important to note that even though the two sets of APIs are designed to be similar, they are not interchangeable. When starting, if the intent is that Spark would be the runtime for a production deployment, it would make sense to start out using Spark locally. The code and logic changes to account for immutability between the different runtimes can be quite a challenge.

Loading the Data

Now that we have wired up the dependencies, we are ready to load our data. This is already uploaded to the cluster, as outlined earlier. We will use Spark's file API to load the FNN data. We also need to specify the encoding, as we have double-wide characters in the data, which fail in Spark:

```
# Load the file
# Use pandas to read CSV
data = pd.read_csv(TRAINING_dataFile, encoding='utf-8')

# peek at the data
data.head(3)
```

Figure 6-12 shows a peek at the structure of the FNN dataset that was loaded.

```
Data columns (total 8 columns):
 #   Column                  Non-Null Count  Dtype
---  ------                  --------------  -----
 0   id                      15212 non-null  int64
 1   date                    15212 non-null  object
 2   speaker                 15212 non-null  object
 3   statement               15212 non-null  object
 4   sources                 15212 non-null  object
 5   paragraph_based_content 15212 non-null  object
 6   fullText_based_content  15212 non-null  object
 7   label_fnn               15212 non-null  object
dtypes: int64(1), object(7)
```

Figure 6-12. FNN training dataset

> It might seem better to use Spark's built-in DataFrames to load the files and possibly load using `spark.read.csv`:
>
> ```
> data = spark.read.csv(fakeNewsFile_training,
>         header=True, inferSchema=True,
>         multiLine=True, escape="\\")
> data.cache()
> ```
>
> However, the FNN dataset, with its nested dictionaries, breaks the parsing. The data is loaded as multiple rows. Specifically, the two fields that get spilled into multiple rows are `paragraph_based_con tent` and `fullText_based_content`.
>
> Pandas is better at parsing this and handling the idiosyncrasies as it pertains to this dataset.

One important distinction when using Pandas compared with Spark is the handling of null in the data. In Pandas this is expressed as a *NaN*, but in Spark, this needs to be expressed as a *None*. This conversion from *NaN* to *None* is not automatic and is something we need to handle. Without this, when we apply labeling functions, using Snorkel later will fail:

```
# Best to avoid pandas in spark but we trying to keep it consistent
# We replace the 'NaN' with 'None' for Spark
data = data.where(cond=data.notna(), other=None)
```

Handling nulls

As we did earlier in Chapter 3, we use the `label_fnn` column and, based on its value, convert it to a number. We need a number instead of a string for validation:

```
data["label_numeric"] = data.apply(
    lambda row: 1 if row["label_fnn"]=='real' else 0, axis=1)

# peek at the data
data.head(3)
```

Note that the result we see in Figure 6-13 shows only a subset for brevity when printed. The following output, however, shows the structure of the DataFrame:

```
Data columns (total 17 columns):
 #   Column                                        Non-Null Count   Dtype
---  ------                                        --------------   -----
 0   id                                            15212 non-null   int64
 1   date                                          15212 non-null   object
 2   speaker                                       15212 non-null   object
 3   statement                                     15212 non-null   object
 4   sources                                       15212 non-null   object
 5   paragraph_based_content                       15212 non-null   object
 6   fullText_based_content                        15212 non-null   object
 7   label_fnn                                      15212 non-null   object
 8   label_numeric                                 15212 non-null   int64
 9   www.politifact.com                             4688 non-null   object
10   www.snopes.com                                  423 non-null   object
11   www.twitter.com                                   3 non-null   object
12   www.factcheck.org                               461 non-null   object
13   factcheck.afp.com                                21 non-null   object
14   www.washingtonpost.com/news/fact-checker        158 non-null   object
15   www.realclearpolitics.com                       120 non-null   object
16   www.glennbeck.com                                22 non-null   object
```

paragraph_based_content	fullText_based_content	label_fnn	label_numeric
['A coalition of government watchdog groups la...	A coalition of government watchdog groups last...	fake	0
['As Supreme Court justices embarked on three ...	As Supreme Court justices embarked on three da...	fake	0
["Here's a new one: The Senate budget committe...	Here's a new one: The Senate budget committee ...	fake	0

Figure 6-13. Converting label to numbers

Fact-Checking Sites

The following remain the same as we saw in Chapter 3:

- The fact-checking sites
- The use of `urllib` package to handle the URLs and read the sites
- The `BeautifulSoup` python package to parse the content of the site

As a reminder, here are the fact-checking sites we used earlier:

- *www.politifact.com*
- *www.snopes.com*
- *www.factcheck.org*
- *factcheck.afp.com*
- *www.washingtonpost.com/news/fact-checker*
- *www.realclearpolitics.com*
- *www.glennbeck.com*

We do need to tweak the `fact_checking_sites()` function to accommodate the need to handle nulls differently and incorporate None:

```
# contacts a URL downloads the website's content and parses it
def get_parsed_html(url):
    req = Request(url, headers={'User-Agent': 'Mozilla/5.0'})
    webpage = urlopen(req).read()
    parsed_html = BeautifulSoup(webpage)
    return parsed_html


fact_checking_sites = {
    "www.politifact.com" : get_politifact_image_alt,
    "www.snopes.com": get_snopes_image_alt,
    "www.twitter.com":  extract_twitter_name,
    "www.factcheck.org": get_factcheck_first_paragraph,
    "factcheck.afp.com": get_factcheck_afp_title,
    "www.washingtonpost.com/news/fact-checker": None,
    "www.realclearpolitics.com": None,
    "www.glennbeck.com": None,
}
```

The functions that check specifics for each site haven't changed from earlier. The following examples show this, but note that we have not shown all of the functions again here for brevity:

```
# www.politifact.com
def get_politifact_image_alt(url):
    result = "abstain"
    try:
        parsed_html = get_parsed_html(url)
        div = parsed_html.body.find('div', attrs={'class':'m-statement__meter'})
        result = div.find("img", attrs={'class':'c-image__original'})["alt"]
    except Exception as e:
        print(e)
    return result


 # www.twitter.com
 def extract_twitter_name(url):
    domain = "https://twitter.com/"
    sub = url[url.find(domain) + len(domain):]
    index = sub.find('/')
    if(index == -1):
        return sub
    else:
        return sub[:index]
```

Once all of the data is loaded, cleaned, and parsed, we only use data that has at least one label. The following filters out any rows that were null:

```
data2 = data[data["www.politifact.com"].notnull()
            | data["www.snopes.com"].notnull()
            | data["www.factcheck.org"].notnull()
            | data["factcheck.afp.com"].notnull()
```

```
            | data["www.realclearpolitics.com"].notnull()
            | data["www.glennbeck.com"].notnull()
            | data["www.washingtonpost.com/news/fact-checker"].notnull()
            | data["www.twitter.com"].notnull()]
```

Transfer Learning Using the LIAR Dataset

Similar to earlier in Chapter 3, we use the LIAR dataset and crowdsourcing to understand patterns of fake versus real statements for speakers and use these patterns to
rate future statements. The underlying premise is that speakers publishing a higher
rate of statements that are thought to be false will have a greater likelihood of con-
tinuing to do that when compared to those speakers that have a higher rate of statements that are classified as true.

We read the LIAR dataset that was uploaded earlier and for Spark's runtime address
missing values, then we mark them as None. Figure 6-14 shows a quick peek to validate the changes once we address the missing value.

```
# Load the LIAR dataset
data3 = pd.read_csv(LIAR_dataFile)

# Clean up the NaNs
data3 = data3.where(cond=data3.notna(), other=None)

# Take a peek at the data to ensure all is correct
data3.head(3)
```

speaker	statement	sources	paragraph_based_content	fullText_based_content	label-liar
Instagram posts	"COVID-19 started because we eat animals"	[https://www.cdc.gov/coronavirus/2019-ncov/ca	["Vegan Instagram users are pinning the 2019 c...	Vegan Instagram users are pinning the 2019 cor...	barely-true
Glenn Beck	Says Michelle Obama has 43 people on her staff.	[http://www.glennbeck.com/2011/02/25/while-wo...	["Glenn Beck rekindled a falsehood about the s...	Glenn Beck rekindled a falsehood about the siz...	pants-fire
Mike Pence	Says President Donald Trump "has signed more l...	[https://nrf.com/events/retail-advocates-summ...	["Vice President Mike Pence says that when it ...	Vice President Mike Pence says that when it co...	half-true

Figure 6-14. Preview of the "fake news detection (LIAR)" dataset

The labels, of course, are the claims that are the output of the Truth-O-Meter values.
We only leverage the claims that are "true," "mostly-true," "false," and "pants-fire." The
labeling function is the same as earlier, and if the speaker has a higher than 60% history of speaking falsehood, this `labeling_function` votes for the article to be FAKE.
Vice versa if the percentage of true claims is higher than 60%:

```
@labeling_function()
def speaker(row):
    speaker = row["speaker"]
    if(speaker in true_percent and true_percent[speaker] > 0.6):
        return REAL
    if(speaker in false_percent and false_percent[speaker] > 0.6):
        return FAKE
    return ABSTAIN
```

Weak Classifiers: Generating Agreement

Snorkel uses a multitask approach (where each task is a labeling function) and evaluates the effectiveness of each task by observing the conflicts between them. As such, the first step in using Snorkel and labeling the data would be to aggregate and resolve any conflicts on the votes from the labeling functions. We will start by splitting the data in a train and validation set with an 80%/20% split, respectively:

```
# Calculate the data size to split for an 80-20 ratio for training & testing
data_size = data.shape[0]
train_data_size = int(data_size*0.8)
```

We use a list of `labeling_functions` and store this in an array called `lfs`. To this dataset, we will use the `SparkLFApplier`, which will execute the labeling functions to evaluate a REAL, a FAKE, or an ABSTAIN vote for each of the labeling functions on each data example.

There are a few important differences when Snorkel runs on Spark compared to running Snorkel on a single machine. First, we need to use a different class—the `SparkLFApplier` instead of the `PandasLFApplier`. The `SparkLFApplier` needs a Spark RDD as an input where each row reflects the data point. And as we saw earlier in the chapter, Spark and Pandas DataFrames are quite different.

Before we can use the `SparkLFApplier` function, we need to get a RDD from a Pandas DataFrame. While this might seem unusual, it is not that uncommon when situations change and we need to scale out to using Spark.

One way to get an RDD from a Pandas DataFrame is to follow this two-step process. First, we convert to a Spark DataFrame, which despite the name is very different from a Pandas DataFrame. Then from that Spark DataFrame, we create an RDD. This resultant RDD is then passed into the `SparkLFApplier.apply()` function, which returns a matrix of labels, as they are emitted by the respective labeling functions:

```
data = data.sample(frac = 1, random_state=1)

lfs = [
        label_rp,
        label_wp,
        label_snopes,
        label_politifact,
        factcheckqa_sentiment,
        factcheckafpqa_sentiment,
        speaker
    ]

# Convert pandas DFs to Spark DFs and then to RDDs
rdd_data = spark.createDataFrame(data).rdd
```

```
# Split the data in an 80-20 ratio for train and test
df_train = data[:train_data_size]
df_train = df_train.where((pd.notnull(df_train)), None)

df_valid = data[train_data_size:]
df_valid = df_valid.where((pd.notnull(df_valid)), None)

# invoke Snorkel
applier = SparkLFApplier(lfs=lfs)
L_train = applier.apply(rdd_data)
LFAnalysis(L=L_train, lfs=lfs).lf_summary()
```

Creating an RDD in Spark

If you use one of the popular ways to create an RDD using the parallelize() function in SparkContext, it will fail:

```
# This will create an RDD as expected, but
# it will fail when called with Snorkel later.
rdd_data = spark.sparkContext.parallelize(df_train)
```

Therefore, we recommend using the createDataFrame() function to create the RDD—and that will work with Snorkel and not fail:

```
# Creating an RDD using this will work.
rdd_data = spark.createDataFrame(data).rdd
rdd_train = spark.createDataFrame(df_train).rdd
rdd_valid = spark.createDataFrame(df_valid).rdd
```

When we run this in our cluster using the earlier data, we get the results, as seen in Figure 6-15. To help understand these results of the output from the labeling functions, we can use the LFAnalysis function to analyze. LFAnalysis are tools from Snorkel that report how our labeling functions perform relative to each other and help us evaluate the performance of the labeling functions.

	j	Polarity	Coverage	Overlaps	Conflicts
label_rp	0	[0, 1]	0.007889	0.006574	0.001906
label_wp	1	[0, 1]	0.010387	0.009400	0.003353
label_snopes	2	[0]	0.027807	0.026887	0.003024
label_politifact	3	[0, 1]	0.126413	0.093479	0.037142
factcheckqa_sentiment	4	[0, 1]	0.020379	0.018998	0.009663
factcheckafpqa_sentiment	5	[0, 1]	0.000986	0.000986	0.000592
speaker	6	[0, 1]	0.717920	0.134236	0.044833

Figure 6-15. SparkLFApplier result—training set

As a reminder, Coverage shows how many data points have at least one label. Overlaps are the percentage of data points with two or more nonabstain labels. And finally, Conflict is the percentage of data points with conflicting labels (which also are non-abstaining).

Looking at the `LFAnalysis` report in Figure 6-15, we have surprisingly high coverage for `label_rp`, `label_wp`, and `label_snopes`, and as a result they also have higher conflicts and overlaps.

Type Conversions Needed for Spark Runtime

Before we can run the training of the model, we need to convert a few data types and shape the dataset to be able to run on Spark.

If you recall, when we split the data into an 80/20 ratio for the training and testing set, that data type is still a Pandas DataFrame (`pandas.core.frame.DataFrame`), and the training dataset looks like what is displayed in Figure 6-16.

	id	date	speaker	statement	sources	paragraph_based_content	fullText_based_content	label_fnn	label_numeric	www.politifact.com	www.snopes.com
3176	1248	2009-10-07T18:19:31-04:00	Michael Moore	During the Reagan era, while productivity incr...	['http://michaelmoore.com/books-films/facts/ca...	['In his new film,', 'Capitalism: A Love Story...	In his new film,\nCapitalism: A Love Story\n...	real	1	None	None
8207	4518	2011-09-29T11:30:57-04:00	Gary Johnson	"It costs more money to put a person on death ...	['http://journals.gmu.edu/index.php/newvoices/...	['Opposition to the death penalty is one of th...	Opposition to the death penalty is one of thos...	real	1	None	None
3152	15972	2018-10-08T10:14:41-04:00	National Republican Congressional Committee	Says that Minnesota Democratic congressional c...	['https://www.youtube.com/watch?time_continue=...	['As the midterm elections draw closer, a warz...	As the midterm elections draw closer, a warzon...	fake	0	None	None
6579	11165	2015-08-06T22:38:38-04:00	Marco Rubio	"This is the most generous country in the worl...	['http://www.dhs.gov/sites/default/files/publi...	['When U.S. Sen. Marco Rubio of Florida addres...	When U.S. Sen. Marco Rubio of Florida addresse...	real	1	mostly-true	None
5558	14613	2017-10-11T11:38:21-04:00	Donald Trump	"Loopholes in current law prevent 'Unaccompani...	['http://www.politico.com/f/?id=0000015e-fe3d-...	['President Donald Trump recently sent Congres...	President Donald Trump recently sent Congress	fake	0	None	None

Figure 6-16. Training dataset

For us to train using Snorkel, we need to convert all the labeling function columns from `int` to `string`. If we don't do this, when we try and run the training later, we will get an arrow optimization error, but the real cause is type conversion failure.

An example of this failure in our test run is shown here:

```
Error: /databricks/spark/python/pyspark/sql/pandas/conversion.py:315:

    UserWarning: createDataFrame attempted Arrow optimization because
    'spark.sql.execution.arrow.pyspark.enabled' is set to true; however,
    failed by the reason below: Unable to convert the field www.snopes.com.

    If this column is not necessary, you may consider dropping it or
    converting to primitive type before the conversion.

    Direct cause: Unsupported type in conversion from Arrow:
    null Attempting non-optimization as
    'spark.sql.execution.arrow.pyspark.fallback.enabled' is set to true.
```

The reason this is failing is that Snorkel is expecting a string:

```
TypeError: field www.politifact.com: Can not merge
    type <class 'pyspark.sql.types.DoubleType'> and
            <class 'pyspark.sql.types.StringType'>
```

Apache Arrow

Apache Arrow (*https://arrow.apache.org*) is a column-oriented in-memory format that can represent both hierarchical and flat data for efficient analytic workloads. A typical RDBMS is a row-oriented implementation where data is stored by rows. A column-oriented structure is one where data is stored by columns rather than rows.

Internally, Spark uses Apache Arrow to transfer the data between Python and JVM. Arrow usage is disabled by default and is something that we need to enable. Of course, we also need to have Apache Arrow (PyArrow) install on all Spark cluster nodes. Arrow can also be used with other libraries such as NumPy and Pandas.

We need to do the following steps for both the training and validation dataset:

- For all the columns we added (which map to the output of a labeling function), we explicitly convert the type to String.
- We ensure the null is handled correctly and represented as None.
- And finally, we convert the Pandas DataFrame to RDDs using spark.createData Frame as outlined earlier.

We can convert both the datatype for the columns as outlined here. The .asType() method is essentially a cast() method that allows us to transform Pandas objects to the specified type and can be handy when wanting to convert a column, as shown here:

```
# Training dataset
df_train[['www.twitter.com',
          'www.politifact.com',
          'www.snopes.com',
          'www.factcheck.org',
          'factcheck.afp.com',
          'www.washingtonpost.com/news/fact-checker',
          'www.realclearpolitics.com',
          'www.glennbeck.com']] =
df_train[['www.twitter.com',
          'www.politifact.com',
          'www.snopes.com',
          'www.factcheck.org',
          'factcheck.afp.com',
          'www.washingtonpost.com/news/fact-checker',
          'www.realclearpolitics.com',
          'www.glennbeck.com']].astype(str)
```

```
# Validation dataset
df_valid[['www.twitter.com',
          'www.politifact.com',
          'www.snopes.com',
          'www.factcheck.org',
          'factcheck.afp.com',
          'www.washingtonpost.com/news/fact-checker',
          'www.realclearpolitics.com',
          'www.glennbeck.com']] =
  df_valid[['www.twitter.com',
            'www.politifact.com',
            'www.snopes.com',
            'www.factcheck.org',
            'factcheck.afp.com',
            'www.washingtonpost.com/news/fact-checker',
            'www.realclearpolitics.com',
            'www.glennbeck.com']].astype(str)
```

Now, with the cleaned-up data types, we can convert these into RDDs:

```
# Training dataset conversion
rdd_train = spark.createDataFrame(df_train).rdd

# Validation dataset conversion
rdd_valid = spark.createDataFrame(df_valid).rdd
```

After the conversion, we are now finally ready to train the model:

```
label_model = LabelModel()

# seed == ultimate question of life
label_model.fit(L_train=L_train, n_epochs=100, log_freq=100, seed=42)

preds_train_label = label_model.predict(L=L_train)
preds_valid_label = label_model.predict(L=L_valid)
L_valid = applier.apply(rdd_valid)

Y_valid = df_valid["label_numeric"].values
LFAnalysis(L_valid, lfs).lf_summary(Y_valid)
```

With the training done, we should analyze the validation set. We will do this using LFAnalysis—similar to how we did this earlier for the training set. The output of Snorkel's analysis for the validation set is shown in Figure 6-17.

	j	Polarity	Coverage	Overlaps	Conflicts	Correct	Incorrect	Emp. Acc.
label_rp	0	[0, 1]	0.007558	0.005587	0.001972	23	0	1.000000
label_wp	1	[0, 1]	0.012488	0.012159	0.004601	38	0	1.000000
label_snopes	2	[0]	0.028262	0.026947	0.002629	77	9	0.895349
label_politifact	3	[0, 1]	0.120933	0.086756	0.033520	224	144	0.608696
factcheckqa_sentiment	4	[0, 1]	0.019717	0.017746	0.009201	37	23	0.616667
factcheckafpqa_sentiment	5	[0, 1]	0.001643	0.001643	0.000986	2	3	0.400000
speaker	6	[0, 1]	0.704568	0.129149	0.041735	1645	499	0.767257

Figure 6-17. SparkLFApplier result—validation set

We also use Snorkel's `LabelModel.score()` function to get industry-standard metrics. This allows us to do a more apples-to-apples comparison between iterations and other models:

```
f1_micro = label_model.score(L_valid, Y_valid, metrics=["f1_micro"])
accuracy = label_model.score(L_valid, Y_valid, metrics=["accuracy"])
recall = label_model.score(L_valid, Y_valid, metrics=["recall"])
precision = label_model.score(L_valid, Y_valid, metrics=["precision"])

print("{} {} {} {}".format(f1_micro, accuracy, recall, precision))
```

As we can see in the following code, in our instance on Spark, all three metrics we want to track are quite decent in the high 70% range, with recall almost at 80%. These are quite similar to the metrics we had earlier in Chapter 3.

```
{'f1_micro': 0.7504401408450704}
{'accuracy': 0.7504401408450704}
{'recall': 0.7962798937112489}
{'precision': 0.7273462783171522}
```

Finally, we combine the training and validation sets and save that data to storage:

```
snorkel_predictions = np.concatenate((preds_train_label,preds_valid_label))
data["snorkel_labels"] = snorkel_predictions

data.to_csv(TRAINED_dataFile, header=True)
```

Summary

In this chapter, we explored the need for scalability and saw the difference between scaling up and out. We introduced Apache Spark and saw how its application design allows us to scale relatively easily. We used the Azure-managed instance of Spark (Azure Databricks) as our instance to keep things simple and to allow us to bootstrap quickly.

In this chapter, we used the FakeNewsNet dataset and the implementation from Chapter 3 to scale from one machine to a Spark-managed cluster running on many machines. Along this journey, we also learned the different configuration setups and changes we needed to make to allow our fake news sample to scale. Many of these are nuances of different runtime and execution environments.

Throughout the chapter, we saw the key code differences that are needed for Snorkel to work. We also saw that DataFrames between Pandas and Spark are quite different, including their handling of nulls. These differences are critical enough to make or break our logic and code, and it is important to be aware of them when designing the solution up front.

The ability to scale is critical and required by most enterprises to be able to use weak supervision in production. The recent advancements with data programming using transfer learning and combining Snorkel have the potential for tremendous business success, and we cannot wait for you to come along with us on this journey.

Index

Azure Computer Vision Service, 76
  deploying, 77
  interacting with, 78
  progress in, 67
  transfer learning for, 113
ComputerVisionClient, creating, 79
conditional independence of labeling functions, 30
conflicts in labeling data, 26, 84, 155
coverage for labeling functions, 84, 155
  analyzing, 23
createDataFrame function, 155
CrossEntropyLoss criterion, 121
crowdsourcing labeling, 12
  FakeNewsNet dataset, 61
  using with LIAR dataset, 153

D
Dask DataFrames, 21
data augmentation
  Snorkel framework, 18
  using Snorkel transformers, 33
    applying transformation functions to dataset, 45-47
    data augmentation through GPT-2 prediction, 39-42
    data augmentation through translation, 42-44
    data augmentation through word removal, 36
data engineering, 11
  costs of, 17
data in AI applications, 15
data parallelism, 133
data preparation
  FakeNewsNet dataset for use with RoBERTa model, 101
  FakeNewsNet dataset, for text classification by ktrain, 92-93
data programming, 11
  accelerating software, 14
  Snorkel framework, 18
    applying labels to datasets, 21
    labeling performance, analyzing, 22-27
    reaching labeling consensus with Label-Model, 29-32
    validation set for labeling, 27
  strategies for improving labeling functions, 32

Databricks
  Azure Databricks documentation, 140
  cloud providers other than Azure, 140
  fake news detection dataset on, 143-159
    fact-checking sites, 151-153
    labeling functions for Snorkel, 145
    loading the data, 149-151
    setting up dependencies, 147
    transfer learning using LIAR dataset, 153
    type conversions needed for Spark runtime, 156
    weak classifiers, generating agreements, 154-156
  Spark versus, 138
  using Azure Databricks to scale, 138-143
    cluster configuration, 141
    cluster setup for weak supervision, 141
DataFrames, 19
  getting an RDD from, 154
  of labeling performance, 22
  Pandas and Dask, 21
  preparing for image tags, 80
  Spark versus Pandas, 149
    handling nulls, 150
DataLoaders, 104, 114
  creating Python iterable over training, validation, and testing images, 117
datasets
  high-quality labeled, high costs of, 1
  imbalanced, dealing with, 93
deep learning, 17
  models with pretrained weights and code, 112
deep learning frameworks, 112
dependencies
  Databricks cluster setup for weak supervision, 141
  setting up for fake news dataset deployed on Databricks cluster, 147
disagreement-based methods (semi-supervised learning), 8
distant supervision, 13
DistilBERT models, 90
  training with ktrain, using FakeNewsNet dataset, 95-97
distributed training, 133

E
EM (expectation-maximization) algorithms, 8

NLP, 88-90
   using Hugging Face and transformers,
      100-109
text dataset, labeling, 49-67
text prediction (GPT-2), 39-42
tokenizing text, 36
   using RoBERTa tokenizer, 102
topic classification, 5
torch.optim.SGD function, 121
torchvision, 114
TorchVision ResNet implementation, 123
TorchVision.Models, 120
train function, 124
training data
   for classifier of prime integers, 19
   getting, 13-16
   in resampled FakeNewsNet dataset, 94
   splitting FakeNewsNet dataset into, 93
training datasets
   displaying class names in, 118
   displaying number of images in, 117
   specifying transformations for, 116
   type conversions for fake news detection
      dataset on Spark, 156
   visualizing training data, 119
training loss, 107
   in fine-tuning pre-trained ResNet-50 model
      plotting the loss, 127
   in fine-tuning pretrained ResNet-50 model,
      126
training models
   getting ResNet-50 model ready for, 121
   need to scale for very large training datasets,
      132
   RoBERTa model, 104-108
   using ktrain to train a DistilBERT model
      using the FakeNewsNet dataset, 95
training, distributed, 133
train_test_split, 93
transductive learning, 9
transfer learning, 8
   for computer vision, 113
   for natural language processing, 88
   using LIAR dataset, 153
transformation functions, 34
   specifying for training, validation, and test-
      ing datasets, 116
transformers, 89-90
   Hugging Face, ktrain support for, 95

Hugging Face-based, BCEWithLogitsLoss
   function, 91
using transformer-based models for text
   classification, 90
using with Hugging Face for text classification, 100-109, 100
   (see also RoBERTa model)
translation, data augmentation through, 42-44
Twitter profile and Botometer score, 63
type conversions for FakeNewsNet dataset on
   Spark runtime, 156

U
undersampling, 94
urllib, 53, 151

V
validation datasets
   for data labeling, 27
   displaying class names in, 118
   displaying number of images in, 117
   image transformations for, 116
   output of SparkLFAnalysis for, 158
   type conversions for fake news detection
      dataset on Spark, 157
validation loss, 107
   in fine-tuning pre-trained ResNet-50 model
      plotting the loss, 127
   in fine-tuning pretrained ResNet-50 model,
      126
vertical scaling, 132
visual object recognition, 111-114
   image features representation, 112
   transfer learning for computer vision, 113
visualizations
   feature visualization of layers of GoogleNet
      trained on ImageNet, 113
   matplotlib, 114
   visualizing training data, 119
visualize_images function, 118

W
weak classifiers, 13
   defining and training in TensorFlow, 71-74
   generating agreement among, 64-67,
      154-156
   from image tags, 76
weak supervision

About the Authors

Wee Hyong Tok has extensive leadership experience leading multidisciplinary teams of program managers, engineers, and data scientists and working on advancing the state-of-the-art in data and AI products at Microsoft. Wee Hyong has worn many hats in his career: developer, program/product manager, data scientist, researcher, technical advisor, and strategist. His range of experience has given him unique superpowers to lead and define the strategy for high-performing data and AI innovation teams. He has built successful global data science and engineering teams, drove innovation, start-up, and strategy programs for AI, and has shipped multiple versions of data and AI products and cloud services.

He is a tech visionary with a background in product management, machine learning/ deep learning, and working on complex engagements with customers. Over the years, he has demonstrated that his early thought-leadership white papers on tech trends have become reality and deeply integrated into many products.

His ability to strategize, turn strategy to execution, and drive customer adoption and success for strategic, global customers has enabled him to make things happen for organizations. Throughout his career, he has been a trusted advisor to the C-suite, from Fortune 500 companies to startups.

Wee Hyong is a sought-after speaker and author of 10 books (translated into Chinese, Korean, and German), and he holds a few patents in data and AI. He has a PhD in computer science, an MSc in computing, and a BSc (first-class honors) in computer science from the National University of Singapore.

You can find him at *https://www.linkedin.com/in/weehyongtok*.

Amit Bahree is an accomplished engineering and technology leader with 25 years experience in technology and the proven ability to build and grow multiple teams. Amit is results-oriented with a strong blend of strategy, technology, engineering, and management delivering business critical solutions for leading organizations.

Amit is passionate and experienced in building great products and great teams that push the boundaries of technology to create innovative experiences and outcomes for our customers. Amit loves combining a mix of ingenuity, engineering, and solving complex real-world problems.

With roots in applied research, Amit strives to be a trusted leader and lifelong learner who operates at the intersection of what is possible and what can be possible and change the market landscape.

At Microsoft, Amit is part of the Azure AI Platform team and responsible for building the next set of AI products and services. Amit collaborates with scientists and researchers at MSR, bringing cutting-edge innovations from research to scale for customers across millions of users using the AI Platform: Azure Cognitive Services, Azure Machine Learning, AI Frameworks, and OpenAI GPT3.

His specialties are product and engineering leadership, machine learning, artificial intelligence, reinforcement learning, responsible AI, digital ethics, bots, robotics, cloud platforms, algorithms, protocols, and hiring and building world-class teams.

In the past, Amit has been responsible for emerging tech, cloud, enterprise architecture, modern engineering, and thought leadership. The emerging tech topics are wide, interesting, and intertwined and include AI, automation, machine learning, extended reality (AR, VR, MR), blockchain, IoT, digital ethics, to name a few.

Amit is a keynote speaker and a published author, and he holds a few patents. Amit holds an MSc in software engineering from University of Oxford and a BSc in computer science from University of Pune.

You can find him at *https://www.linkedin.com/in/amitbahree* and on Twitter @bahree (*https://twitter.com/bahree*).

Senja Filipi has over a decade of experience as a software engineer, half of it working in full stack ML applications. In the past, Senja has been part of the team that showcased how Azure and machine learning technologies can be leveraged together to create end-to-end solutions for real case scenarios. She has actively contributed to the open source machine learning ML.NET framework, as well as its UI interface, the ML Model builder.

Senja is currently working on interleaving traditional software with ML models, developing software 2.0 on the AI team.

She holds an MSc in computer science and engineering from the University of Washington and an MSc and a BSc in computer engineering from the Polytechnic University of Tirana.

You can find her at *https://www.linkedin.com/in/senja-filipi*.

Colophon

The animal on the cover of *Practical Weak Supervision* is a yellow warbler (*Setophaga petechia*). These strikingly yellow birds are commonly found across North America, particularly along watercourses and wetlands. For most of the year, they live in trees such as willows, alders, and cottonwoods but migrate to the mangroves of Mexico, Peru, and Brazil during the winter months.

Yellow warblers are small, evenly proportioned birds with straight thin tails and rounded heads. As their name suggests, they're egg-yolk yellow with reddish streaks on their underside, and the distinct coloring on their unmarked face accentuates their large black eyes. The bright birds differ only slightly across regions. In other parts of the world like the mangrove forests of Central and South America, the yellow warbler subspecies have a bright chestnut crown over their head, hence earning the name "golden" yellow warbler.

They can often be found near the tops of tall shrubs and short trees in open, cup-like nests, where cowbirds may also lay their eggs. Yellow warblers try to discourage this by building a new floor over the cowbird eggs and laying their own eggs on that level. They continue to create as many nest floors as the times the cowbirds return to lay their eggs just to thwart them. The warbler's diet usually includes insects and foliage that it gains from foraging with quick hops along small branches and twigs.

Yellow warblers can also be identified by their unique sweet whistled songs. A familiar sound in willows and woodland edges, the males sing various songs, some of which resemble those of the magnolia or chestnut-sided warbler. Currently, the conservation status of the yellow warblers is of least concern because their affinity to second growth and edges makes them less vulnerable to loss of habitat. Many of the animals on O'Reilly covers are endangered; all of them are important to the world.

The cover illustration is by Karen Montgomery, based on a black-and-white engraving from Shaw's *Zoology*. The cover fonts are Gilroy Semibold and Guardian Sans. The text font is Adobe Minion Pro; the heading font is Adobe Myriad Condensed; and the code font is Dalton Maag's Ubuntu Mono.

O'REILLY®

There's much more where this came from.

Experience books, videos, live online training courses, and more from O'Reilly and our 200+ partners—all in one place.

Learn more at oreilly.com/online-learning

Lightning Source UK Ltd.
Milton Keynes UK
UKHW030242191121
394166UK00003B/8